DEPRAVED
ENGLISH

DEPRAVED
ENGLISH

Peter Novobatzky

&

Ammon Shea

St. Martin's Press ❧ New York

DEPRAVED ENGLISH. Copyright © 1999 by Peter Novobatzky and Ammon Shea. All rights reserved. Printed in the United States of America. No part of this book may be used or reproduced in any manner whatsoever without written permission except in the case of brief quotations embodied in critical articles or reviews. For information address St. Martin's Press, 175 Fifth Avenue, New York, N.Y. 10010.

Library of Congress Cataloging-in-Publication Data

Novobatzky, Peter.
    Depraved English / Peter Novobatzky and Ammon Shea. —1st U.S. ed.
        p.   cm.
    Includes bibliographical references (p. 159).
    ISBN 0–312–20773–5
    1. English language—Terms and phrases.   2. English language—Terms and phrases Humor.   3. English language Glossaries, vocabularies, etc.   4. Vocabulary Humor.   I. Shea, Ammon.   II. Title.
    PE1689.N68   1999
    423'.1—dc21   99–26421

First Edition: August 1999

10   9   8   7   6   5   4   3   2   1

For our parents

INTRODUCTION

Amidst the grand panoply that is the English language, the largest on this Earth, tongue of Shakespeare, Byron, and Melville, there are a puzzling number of words that mean "to spray with shit."

In fact, the English language abounds in obscure—and hilarious—sexual, insulting, and disgusting words. Marvelous words, like *bescumber, merkin*, and *pizzle*, that most educated people have never heard of. To date, no one has written a lexicon exclusively devoted to such "depraved" English; the current volume intends to rectify this omission.

Researching this book required no small degree of dedication and sacrifice. Indeed, were the average reader to venture upon such a task, it is very likely that insanity would be the painful result. Only because the authors are compulsive word enthusiasts—willing, among other things, to spend hundreds of hours reading dictionaries from cover to cover—was the undertaking possible at all.

We have dug deeply for these gems, culling them from modern dictionaries, both general and specialized, and rescuing them from the bowels of a variety of out-of-print tomes: lexicons, glossaries, and cyclopedias where they have languished, in some cases, for centuries. Some, until now, have been known to only a few professionals in narrow fields. Others have been neglected over the years, handled with lexicographical distaste by prudish editors and included only begrudgingly in dictionaries, often accompanied by oblique definitions or dismissive labels like "low," "colloquial," "archaic," "vulgar," "obsolete," or "dialect." They are all first-rate words, however, and we present them to the reader with pride.

These words are a part of your legacy as a speaker of English. They are buried treasures to be unearthed, dusted off, and displayed. But unlike in a museum, where the treasures are kept under glass, you are encouraged to handle these curios. Say them; use them. Feel the power in them as they roll off your tongue. They are your birthright.

Many of the words contained in this volume are readily applicable in everyday life. And they are so much more specific and exciting than the old, hackneyed, four-letter standbys so often relied upon. Use them to describe the world around you, or to articulate your own unique depraved notions. Practice saying them a few times and your daily vocabulary will be significantly enriched. Share this book with friends and loved ones and your discourse will elevate to previously inaccessible planes of clarity, exactitude, and vulgarity.

While it is true that a startling proportion of these words describe acts of sexual deviancy, medical abnormalities, things scatological, and outdated farm practices, there is no need for concern. The authors are not obsessed with such matters. It is simply because these areas happen to be such fertile sources of depravity that they are so heavily represented here.

When confronted with this glossary for the first time, typical reactions of early readers have ranged from bemused disbelief to complete denial. Rest assured, dear reader: all of our entries are actual, legitimate English words. There is to our knowledge—and according to the most assiduous and painstaking research—neither a single piece of slang nor a solitary neologism among them.

The words contained in this book were judged worthy of inclusion on many different grounds. Some were lascivious, some were mildly derogatory, and others were utterly revolting. A few were all of these things. There are words—*feague* comes to mind—for objects, practices, and states of being many never knew existed, and words like *frottage*, which describe things one may have known existed but never knew there was a word for. *Jumentous* and *urinous* are useful for describing everyday occurrences, while *copremesis* is more . . . esoteric. But they are all real words, and we have dreamed up the sample sentences so the reader can see them in action.

The time has come to inject new blood into the stale body of English-speaking vulgarity. So use these words! They are amusing, but they are also valuable for other reasons. After all, a vast and inexhaustible vocabulary is a hallmark not only of education, but of innate intelligence as well. Hereafter, when attacked, every reader will be able to seize the intellectual high ground by avoiding a common means of expression in favor of something more elegant and nobler of pedigree.

A NOTE ON
THE ENTRIES

The pronunciation guides that follow each entry are designed for ease of use. However, they are only guides. The way words are pronounced changes with time and region, and even the most authoritative sources are not always in perfect agreement on this topic. Instead of listing multiple pronunciations for a single word, for the sake of simplicity we have selected the single most standard and prevalent one. And, to be frank, in one or two cases (the guttural *frottage*, for example, which we show as rhyming with *cottage*) we have chosen a lesser-known pronunciation.

Similarly, when the sources disagree as to the definition or spelling of a given word, or where multiple definitions exist, we have exercised whatever common sense and lexicographical judgment has been granted us by the fates.

A

aboiement /ah bwah MAHN/ n ❧ Involuntary blurting of animal noises, such as barking.

"The personal ad read simply, 'Handsome SWM, financially secure, seeks SWF for romance, possibly more. **Aboiement** a +,' but Marjorie knew immediately that she had stumbled upon her perfect mate."

achilous /uh KAI lus/ adj ❧ Having no lips.

One of many words scattered throughout this book that are useful for describing common turnoffs.

"Wanda was a wonderful lady, but no matter what her attributes, J. B. could never bring himself to kiss an **achilous** woman."

acokoinonia /uh ko koy NO nee uh/ n ❧ Sex without passion.

Otherwise known as "the doldrums." Or, for some unlucky marrieds, "as good as it gets."

compare **artamesia**

Acokoinonia

acrocephalic /AK ro sef AL ik/ adj ❧ Having a pointed skull.

With a bit of figurative license, this word may be extended to cover anything that might be called "pinheaded," which gives it a very wide range indeed. For example, if you wish to tell someone that his idea is harebrained, tell him it is **"acrocephalic,** plain and simple."

"Rabbi Abramson was a devout and patient man, but the carnival sideshow wedding frustrated even him: after all, how *do* you put a yarmulke on an **acrocephalic** Jew?"

adipocere /AD ip ose eer/ n ✺ A fatty, waxlike material that human and animal tissues sometimes convert into when corpses decompose underwater, and which may preserve physical features for long periods.

Adipocere may be one of the the most bizarre and ghoulish words in the language.

"Freddie Barbarossa, the cemetery king, started out at the bottom, shovel in hand and **adipocere** on his shoes."
compare **gobbets**

agastopia /ag uh STOPE ee uh/ n ✺ The admiration of a part of someone's body.

Everyone occasionally comes under the spell of **agastopia.** Those who do not wish to advertise the condition may purchase a serviceable pair of dark sunglasses from their local five-and-dime store.

It is a proven fact that people who frequently experience **agastopia** are far more likely to fall down open manholes than the population as a whole.
compare **apodyopsis**

agelast /AJ uh last/ n ✺ A person who never laughs.

"Much to the dismay of Baffo, the drugstore-robbing clown, the sentencing judge was a stern **agelast.**"

agrexophrenia /uh GREX o FREE nee uh/ n ✺ Inability to perform sexually due to a fear of being overheard.

"Raising a large family in a quaint little Irish cottage,

agrexophrenia was a continual problem for Mr. and Mrs. McDougal, as the clan usually slept four to a bed."

algolagnia /al go LAG nee uh/ n ✇ The garnering of sexual thrills by inflicting or suffering pain.

"Biff's closet **algolagnia** compelled him to partake in contact sports such as tackle football and rugby, where he quickly earned a reputation as both a glutton for punishment and a sadistic bastard."

compare **mastigophoric**

allochezia /al o KEE zee uh/ n ✇ Defecation from somewhere other than the anus. Also, defecation of something other than feces.

"Nick was suspicious of doctors as a rule, but when his **allochezia** failed to clear up by itself he decided to schedule an appointment."

compare **copremesis, lientery**

amastia /ay MAST ee uh/ n ✇ Lack of breasts.

"He was a born con man who got his start in crime as a teenager, hustling a vile-tasting potion which he claimed could cure **amastia**."

compare **micromastia**

amatorculist /am at or COOL ist/ n ✇ A pitiful or insignificant lover.

From the Latin *amatorculus* (a little, sorry lover).

"Colleagues of Dr. Schiff privately agreed that being dubbed 'the **amatorculist**' by the nursing staff was probably what had precipitated his unfortunate breakdown in the emergency room."

compare meupareunia

ambeer /AM beer/ n 🕊 The spit-out juice from chewing tobacco.

"Being a bat boy was a dream come true for Jimmy, but he soon found that dodging the streams of **ambeer** in the dugout took a lot of practice."

compare sputative

ambodexter /AM buh dex ter/ n 🕊 A corrupt juror; a juror who takes money from both sides.

"Carolyn pocketed the cash and shook her head in amazement: if she had known that being an **ambodexter** was so lucrative, she wouldn't have dodged jury duty all those years."

amychesis /am ik EE sis/ n 🕊 Involuntary scratching of a partner's back during sex.

"As she daubed her wounds with peroxide in the motel bathroom, Charlotte cursed her luck for having taken a lover who suffered from **amychesis**, and began working on what she would tell her husband this time."

anaphrodisiac */an af ro DEE zhee ak/* adj ❧ Suppressing or eliminating sexual desire. n ❧ Something that acts against sexual desire.

"The two women—both in their early thirties and utterly unattractive—scored a hit with their best-seller *The Drools,* which detailed everything women found **anaphrodisiac** about men."

androphilic */an dro FIL ik/* adj ❧ Preferring men over animals.

"Aunt Lucille was a gracious hostess, but she was getting on in years, so at tea everyone pretended not to notice the frenzied and insistent leg-humpings of Winston, her **androphilic** schnauzer."

anile */AN ile/* adj ❧ Old-womanish.

"Montigew wanted very much to play with the other boys, but his attempts to throw a baseball were so **anile** that he wound up skipping rope with the girls again."

anililagnia */uh NIL ih LAG nee uh/* n ❧ Sexual attraction to elderly women.

"Mortimer felt as though he was cursed by the gods: he had finally come to grips with his **anililagnia**, but now his lovers kept dying on him."

compare gerontophilia

anilingus /ay nil ING us/ n ❧ Sexual contact between mouth and anus.

While this word may not be your cup of tea, **anilingus** is evidently enjoyed by enough people to warrant inclusion in a number of fine dictionaries.

"Melvin had always been the office brownnoser, but when the new management team arrived he stepped up his act to full-fledged **anilingus**."

compare **lecheur**

anility /uh NIL it ee/ n ❧ Old-womanishness.

"After the candidate's disastrous performance on national television, it was Peterson's unenviable duty as campaign manager to remind him that **anility** was not what most people looked for in a leader."

anisomastia /an iss o MAST ee uh/ n ❧ The state of having breasts of unequal size.

"Hedda was sold on surgery for her **anisomastia**; the only question was whether to go for enlargement, reduction, or a little of both."

anoia /uh NOY uh/ n ❧ Idiocy.

Paradoxically, a condition most annoying to those who do not suffer from it.

anorchous /an OR kus/ adj ❧ Having no testicles.

" 'Had you not been such an **anorchous** jellyfish,'

shrieked Sheila, Kevin's shrill and over-educated wife, '*you* would have gotten the promotion!' "

anorchus /*an OR kus*/ n ❧ A man with no testicles.

"Only after the humiliating incident with the waiter did it finally dawn on Louisa that she had married a total **anorchus**."

compare **triorchid**

apistia /*uh PISS tee uh*/ n ❧ Marital infidelity.

"Johann was a sly and crafty fellow: having inserted a clause in his prenuptial agreement asserting that **apistia** could not be considered grounds for alimony, he now was free to whore his way about town with complete abandon."

compare **bedswerver**

apodyopsis /*ap o die OP sis*/ n ❧ The act of imagining someone naked.

"There were times, such as the summer he worked at the nursing home, when Wendell found his compulsive **apodyopsis** more of a curse than a blessing."

arrhenopiper /*uh REN o pipe er*/ n ❧ "One that looks lewdly at men," as defined by Joseph T. Shipley in his *Dictionary of Early English*.

A word that well deserves resurrection.

"Cadwaller's buttocks clenched tightly, as they always

did whenever he had to pass through the gaggle of boisterous **arrhenopipers** blocking the men's room."

compare **gynopiper**

artamesia /art uh MEE zhee uh/ n 🌶 Sexual dissatisfaction in a woman due to the premature climax of her partner.

It is a beautiful thing that a word exists for this all-too-common occurrence. There is a difference of opinion, however, as to where the word **artamesia** comes from. According to J. E. Schmidt, author of *The Lecher's Lexicon,* the roots are from the Greek *artao* (to hang) and *mesos* (in the middle). While this explanation is both plausible and amusing, one cannot ignore the case to be made for Artimesia, the ancient Greek queen of Helicarnassus, as the eponymous root of the word.

According to the history books, Artimesia was exceedingly fond of a youth named Darnadus, and when he rebuffed her licentious advances she tore his eyes from his head as he slept (you go, girlfriend!!!). Yet a third possibility is that the word originates with Artemesia Gentileschi (1593–1653), a renowned Italian painter. Her most famous painting, *Judith and Maidservant with the Head of Holofernes*, happens to depict two women who have decapitated a man who has slept with one of them.

So there are three viable explanations—which hardly matters, really, for if you're experiencing **artamesia** you need more than a good etymology.

compare **acokoinonia**

aspermia /*ay SPERM ee uh*/ n ❧ Inability to ejaculate semen.

"Ironically, the very same **aspermia** that rendered Hedley's sexual efforts futile for him also led to his gaining a reputation as a tireless love machine."

compare **spermatoschesis**

asshead /*ASS hed*/ n ❧ A blockhead; a stupid person.

While **asshead** has the ring of a modern-day schoolyard taunt, it actually has a long and noble history as a legitimate insult. As such, it has a certain blunt and potent charm.

axunge /*AX unj*/ n ❧ Medicinal lard prepared from geese or pigs.

Good for what ails ye!

"Sales of the new minestrone soup did not benefit from the consumer group's announcement that 'natural flavorings' was really just a fancy name for **axunge**."

❦ B ❧

baculum /BAK yoo lum/ n ❧ The penis bone; present in many mammals, absent in humans.

Thank God.

"Although he traveled in the highest social circles, Tully was regarded as something of an eccentric, perhaps because of his extensive **baculum** collection."

balanic /buh LAN ik/ adj ❧ Having to do with the penis or clitoris.

"Sigmund E. Hopfeizer, M.D., was irked: didn't his generous donation to his alma mater warrant a slightly more prominent acknowledgment than a plaque in the Hall of **Balanic** Studies?"

balanoplasty /buh LAN o plass tee/ n ❧ Plastic surgery of the penis.

"When his doctor enthusiastically recommended drastic **balanoplasty** to cure his slight incontinence, Arthur knew it was time to get a second opinion."

syn **phalloplasty**

bariatrics /*barry AT rix*/ n, pl ⁓ The field of medicine concerned with obesity.

"As he lay on the floor of the sauna in his rubber suit, moments before lapsing into unconsciousness, Milton reflected that the science of **bariatrics** still had a long way to go."

compare **impinguinate**

bastinado /*bass tin AY do*/ v ⁓ To beat the soles of someone's feet with a stick or club. n ⁓ The practice of beating the soles of the feet with a stick or club.

"Talk about dedication: Luigi worked full time during the week as flogger and executioner, but somehow still found time enough to take **bastinado** classes on the weekends."

compare **ferule**, **pandy**

bathycolpian /*bath ik ALL pee an*/ adj ⁓ Having deep cleavage.

There are so many banal expressions for this particular concept that our language is crying out for a resurrection of the proper terminology. Very few women out there enjoy the salutation "nice rack!" or relish compliments on their "bazookas." And while a statement like "Your **bathycolpian** state overwhelms and delights me" may not pave the way to romance on its own, at least it's less likely to get you slapped.

"There was a moment of confusion during the inter-

Bathycolpian

view on the Capitol steps, when the senator's hearing aid fell down the front of the **bathycolpian** reporter's blouse."

compare **mammose**

bdellatomy /*del AT o mee*/ n ❧ The cutting of a leech while it is sucking, in order to increase the flow of blood from the patient.

Apparently plain old leeching just wasn't disgusting enough to cure everybody.

"As a young surgeon, Clarence soon learned not to assign names to his leeches; it only made it harder for him when the time came for a **bdellatomy**."

bdolotic /*DOLL uh tik*/ adj ❧ Prone to farting.

What can we say about **bdolotic**, except that its usefulness as a word is obvious.

"To the horror of her hapless niece, old Mrs. Grubowski not only grew more and more violently drunk as the evening progressed, but increasingly **bdolotic**, as well."

compare **carminative, flatus, meteorism**

bedswerver / *BED swerv er*/ n ❧ An unfaithful spouse.

A more visually expressive term for a cheating mate is hard to find. **Bedswerver** conjures up the image of a husband or wife walking toward the conjugal bed, then at the last possible moment thinking "Naaah," and changing direction midstride.

compare **apistia**

beldam /BELL dam/ n 🦚 A mean and ugly old woman.

"Bartholemew was blessed with scant physical courage: in fact, he lived in constant fear of the **beldam** across the hall with the yippy poodle."

beray /bee RAY/ v 🦚 To splatter with feces.

"After getting **berayed** yet again, Ted the zookeeper made a grim vow: one day he would get even with those damn monkeys."

> syn **bescumber, conskite, immerd**
> compare **ordurous, sharny, shitten**

bescumber /bee SCUM ber/ v 🦚 To splatter with feces; to spray with ordure.

This graphic, horrible-sounding verb is often applicable in life. Remember the bathroom stall in Grand Central Station that time you absolutely *couldn't* wait? Was it not **bescumbered** from floor to eye level, challenging your knowledge of human anatomy and/or the laws of physics?

> syn **beray, conskite, immerd**
> compare **ordured, sharny, shitten**

beslobber /bee SLOB er/ v 🦚 To cover with sloppy kisses. Also, to befoul with spittle or anything else running from the mouth.

That covers everything from orange juice to—well, more exotic liquids.

❧ *Bespew* ❧

"Balthazar reached to his pocket, then groaned inwardly: why was it that he could never remember to bring a spare handkerchief on these dates with his **beslobbering** new girlfriend Estelle?"

compare **conspue**

bespew /bee SPEW/ v ⮞ To eject vomit upon.

"It was another one of those nights for the Jenkinses: getting drunk, fighting viciously, making up, making love, and, inevitably, **bespewing** each other before it was all over."

bezoar /BEE zore/ n ⮞ A hardened hair ball found in the digestive tracts of grazing animals, sometimes rumored to have medicinal use.

Every man of the world should have a few of these lying around—perhaps for use as paperweights.

"On the steppes of Old Mother Russia we had no baseballs, but more than once of an afternoon we would go out and toss the old **bezoar** around."

bilious /BILL ee us/ adj ⮞ Suffering from an overflow of bile from the liver, with symptoms including headache, indigestion, furry tongue, and lethargy.

"Fifteen straight nights of drinking had resulted in the superintendent's present **bilious** condition—he was definitely in no shape to clean the sewer drain."

compare **crapulent**

❧ Blissom ❧

blattoid /BLAT oid/ adj 🖎 Resembling a cockroach.

"Duane was a legend as an exterminator, in part because he could really think like those he was hired to kill, and as the years rolled on he became more and more **blattoid** himself."

compare suoid

blennorrhea /blen uh REE uh/ n 🖎 The morbid and excessive secretion of mucus.

When every corner of every tissue in the house has been used twice, the toilet paper is ancient history, the sore area under your nose resembles a pink toothbrush moustache, and your nostrils are plugged with wads of shredded dinner napkin, then you know that **blennorrhea** is upon you.

blissom /BLISS um/ v 🖎 To copulate with a ewe; said of rams (and, less frequently, shepherds). adj 🖎 In heat; ready to be **blissomed.**

This little charmer sounds like it should mean something sweet and ethereal, like "blossom" or "blessing," and perhaps it does, in its own way. However, if one reads in the culture section of the paper about a "**blissoming** young talent on the downtown arts scene," one may be reasonably if not entirely sure that a printing error is to blame.

"Having **blissomed** the ewe, Calvert found himself strangely devoid of any hint of remorse."

compare brim

bolus /*BO lus*/ n 🐦 A ball of chewed food, ready to be swallowed. Also, something hard to swallow, such as a big pill.

"The enormous **bolus** in his cheek oscillated slightly as he spoke, but Cleon showed no sign of getting ready to swallow it and continued his lengthy monologue."

bonnyclabber /*BON ee klab er*/ n 🐦 Milk gone sour; thickened, curdled milk. Also, beer mixed with buttermilk or sour cream.

Bonnyclabber comes from the Irish *bainne* (milk) + *claba* (thick mud). One sees the word shortened to *clabber,* with no change in meaning. Milk that has turned is said to be *clabrous.*

"Experimentation proved beyond a doubt what Winston had suspected all along: pounding **bonnyclabber** was not an effective hangover remedy."

borborygmus /*bor bor IG muss*/ n 🐦 A rumbling in the intestines caused by gas.

"Andy, the chaplain, was a true professional, and when the sacred silence of the prayer circle was shattered by the severe **borborygmus** of one of his flock, he continued with his benediction without missing a beat."

compare **flatus**

brim /*BRIM*/ v 🐦 To be in heat. Also, to copulate (said of swine).

"With a deep feeling of pride and satisfaction, Larsen

inhaled the fresh morning air and surveyed his little farm: the cows lowing in the fields, the sheep grazing on the hill, the swine **brimming** furiously in their pens."

compare **blissom**

bromidrosiphobia /bro mih dro sif O bee uh/ n 🍵 A hallucinatory fear of body odor.

One of only two phobias included in this book (out of a possible five hundred or more). **Bromidrosiphobia** is interesting because it carries with it the odd notion of olfactory hallucinations. Just what does one do with a **bromidrosiphobe**—shake him by the shoulders and tell him he's smelling things again?

bromidrosis /bro mid RO sis/ n 🍵 Ill-smelling sweat.

"Russell never quite made the big time as a professional wrestler, his trick of overcoming opponents with his **bromidrosis** apparently failing to captivate audiences."

compare **kakidrosis, maschalephidrosis, podobromhidrosis**

bromomenorrhea /BRO mo men o REE uh/ n 🍵 Foul-smelling menstrual discharge.

Vile, loathsome, and until now, unmentionable.

"The day they started advertising **bromomenorrhea** remedies during the evening news, Mr. Pendleton finally threw his television away."

compare **stomatomenia**

Burke

bromopnea /*bro MOP nee uh*/ n ❧ Foul-smelling breath.

"Dr. Hubbard was a bit of a mystery to us at the clinic: as a dentist he was a genius with a drill, yet he couldn't seem to cure his own horrid **bromopnea**."

compare **saprostomus**

buccula /*BUK yoo luh*/ n ❧ A loose, saggy mass of flesh underneath the chin; a double chin.

"Many were the tossings and turnings that night in the Carpathian village, as the sleepless peasants cowered in their beds from fear of becoming the next victim of the evil Count **Buccula**, world's portliest vampire."

syn **choller**

burke /*BURK*/ v ❧ To murder by smothering; originally, in order to sell the corpse to a medical school.

So called after William Burke, the diabolical nineteenth-century Edinburgh killer who suffocated his victims and sold their unblemished corpses to medical schools for dissection.

Also, figuratively, to "kill" something quietly or furtively behind the scenes: to **burke** an investigation, for example.

byental /*by ENT ull*/ n ❧ A horse's penis.

Or, as the *Oxford English Dictionary* puts it: "The yard of a horse."

This word is hereby brought to your attention so you

don't end up ordering the fricasseed **byental** while on your eating tour of provincial England (at least not without being fully informed).

compare pizzle

Byental

C

cacocallia /kak o KAL ee uh/ n ✒ The state of being ugly but sexy.

Warning: The authors strongly advise against using this word as a compliment.

cagamosis /kag uh MO sis/ n ✒ An unhappy or unpleasant marriage.

Considering how common the thing is which it describes, it is surprising that the word **cagamosis** is not more widely known. Alas, even divorce lawyers, the particular group that transforms the misfortunes of unhappy marriages into fortunes for themselves, are probably overwhelmingly ignorant of the very word that lines their larders.

callipygian /kal ip EYE gee an/ adj ✒ Having nicely shaped buttocks.

From the Greek *kallos* (beautiful) + *pyge* (buttocks).

The noun form of this word is **callipyge** (a person with nicely shaped buttocks).

compare **dasypygal, pygobombe, steatopygous**

Cagamosis

~ Caprylic ~

caprylic /*kuh PRILL ik*/ adj ~ Evocative of a rank and fetid goat (said of smells).

"Brush in hand and tears in his eyes, Horatio made a mental note not to let the hardware store man talk him into buying **caprylic** paint ever again."

syn **hircine**

compare **rammish**

carminative /*kar MIN uh tiv*/ adj ~ Relieving flatulence; acting to expel wind from the body. n ~ An agent that relieves flatulence by helping to expel wind from the body.

"Doug was talking to his pretty young boss when two things happened: the **carminative** prescribed for his indigestion took hold, and the elevator broke down."

compare **bdolotic, flatus, meteorism**

caseate /*KAY see ate*/ v ᵔ To become cheesy; be subject to **caseation**.

When someone asks you what you think of the new best-seller you wasted good money buying, tell them the book **caseates** in the second half, and you might feel a bit better.

caseation /*kay see AY shun*/ n ᵔ Conversion into cheese. Also, a morbid condition whereby flesh develops a cheesy appearance and consistency.

As with **caseate,** the best way to employ this potentially useful word is to think of "cheesy" as meaning crummy, corny, and tacky. Then you can apply **caseation** not only to substances like curd and flesh (ugh), but to things that deeply offend all amateur culture critics, such as screenplays that undergo a rapid and thorough process of **caseation** after being purchased by major Hollywood studios.

catarolysis /*kat uh RALL ih sis*/ n ᵔ The practice of cursing to let off steam.

"Denied the outlet of a prolonged **catarolysis** when things went wrong, Blake had a massive stroke and died shortly after making the amazing career switch from truck driver to beloved host of a live children's television show."

compare **coprolalia**

ceruminosis /SEH roo min O sis/ n ~ The excessive secretion of **cerumen** (ear wax).

"Davey's parents breathed a sigh of relief: the sullen behavior, the bad grades, the loud music—**ceruminosis,** not Satan worship, was to blame."

chankings /CHAN kings/ n, pl ~ Slightly masticated spat-out food, such as olive pits or gristle.

Chankings are a part of life, and it is high time they were recognized as such. The stubborn refusal of hosts and hostesses to provide suitable receptacles for their guests' **chankings** is a mark of careless incivility, even boorishness. After all, who feels comfortable balling up napkin after napkin of herring bones and sunflower seed husks? At the next function you attend, request a bowl for **chankings** in a polite and debonair fashion, and when one is delivered you'll be able to dispose of your cherry pits with an air of impeccable cultivation.

cholagogic /kall uh GOG ik/ adj ~ Producing a flow of bile.

With a little liberty of usage, this medical term can be applied to such diverse phenomena as newpaper editorials, traffic jams, and modern architecture.

choller /CHALL er/ n ~ Fat, pendulous flesh hanging from the lower jaw; double chin.

"Every morning the same dilemma for Mr. Pinkerton, the overnourished banker: should he button his collar above or below his massive **choller**?"

syn buccula

chordee /*kore DEE*/ n ❧ Painful downward curving of the erect penis, happening especially at night; sometimes a side effect of gonnorrhea.

Also known as *phallocamposis*.

"Jenkins, the portly exhibitionist, might never have been picked out of the police lineup had his severe **chordee** not given him away."

compare priapism

chyme /*KIME*/ n ❧ Partially digested liquid food.

"Rosemary's filthy-drunk roomate had ruined yet another dish with her careless vomitings: after all, the recipe called for parsley, sage, and *thyme,* not **chyme**."

compare lientery

cicisbeo /*sih SIZZ bee o*/ n ❧ The young male lover/escort/admirer of a married woman.

Basically, a **cicisbeo** is the paramour of a married lady, although the definition is imprecise. Italian in origin, the word covers the spectrum of male admirers, from occasional hangers-on to full-fledged lovers.

claqueur /klak IRRH/ n ✒ A member of a **claque** (a mob of hired applauders). Also, figuratively, any sycophantic yes-man.

Whether they get money or just free tickets, it doesn't matter—**claqueurs** are the mainstay of infomercials and insipid little talk shows. Do they have no shame?
compare **saulie**

clyster /KLY ster/ v ✒ To administer an enema. n ✒ An enema.

✒ *Clyster* ✒

"Paul's penchant for administering irrigations on the flimsiest pretense led to his being dubbed 'the **clyster meister**' by his fellow nurses."

compare huskanoy

collywobbles /*KALL ee wob ulls*/ n, pl 🐾 Intestinal distress characterized by cramping and diarrhea.

"Not a working bathroom in the whole department store, and a severe case of the **collywobbles:** Parker had to get creative—fast!"

colpoxerosis /*kole po zeh RO sis*/ n 🐾 extreme dryness of the vagina.

Another medical term with its uses in everyday life.

"Vivian was immediately removed as editor of the school newspaper when officials caught wind of her upcoming article: Overcoming **Colpoxerosis** on Prom Night—What Every Girl Needs to Know."

compare vaginismus

conskite /*kun SKITE*/ v 🐾 To besplatter with dung.

"Darius, creative director of the Circus Maximus, sighed dejectedly: all the mobs ever wanted was blood, blood, and more blood. Why, even his attempt to inject comedy into the show by having the prisoners **conskited** by wild animals had flopped miserably."

syn beray, bescumber, immerd
compare ordured, sharny, shitten

conspue /kun SPEW/ v ✒ To spit on with contempt.

"As he stood on line for yet another unemployment check, Pendleton sighed and once again reflected that **conspuing** his boss's wife had been something of a miscalculation."

✒ *Contrectation* ✒

contrectation /kon trek TAY shun/ n ✒ Touching and fingering, as in the initial stages of lovemaking. Also, a pathological urge to fondle all members of the opposite sex.

Contrectation describes the same root action (touching) in two very different contexts: primarily associated with tender lovers, the word moonlights in conjunction with drooling sex maniacs.

"As if Julius's **contrectation** weren't frustrating enough to deal with on its own, after the skiing accident he was confined to a full body cast and attended to by a squadron of buxom young nurses."

copracrasia /KOPE ruh KRAY zhuh/ n ꙮ Involuntary defecation.

"Like it or not, it was **copracrasia** that set Merdy, the famous baggy-pants comedian, on his road to fame and fortune."

syn **encopresis**

copremesis /kope rem EE sis/ n ꙮ The condition of being so constipated that one vomits one's own feces.

Sorry, but **copremesis** is not a word for the weak of stomach. When confronted with this little sparkler, most people say something like "No! That can't happen!" Well, it can happen, and does. The mere thought is enough to make even the most hardened logophiles put down their forks. So when you go to bed tonight, give thanks to the god of your choice that it hasn't happened to you.

compare **allochezia**

coprolagnia /KOPE ro LAG nee uh/ n ❧ Erotic gratification from handling or smelling feces.

"In her third year of medical school, Lisa finally yielded to her latent **coprolagnia** and signed up for several courses in proctology."

coprolalia /kope ruh LAY lee uh/ n ❧ Pathological indecency of language; also, sexual gratification from indecent language.

"Claiming that his **coprolalia** was an affliction, not merely a bad habit, Swanson sued and regained his post as headmaster of the boarding school."

compare **catarolysis**

coprolite /KOP ro lite/ n ❧ Fossilized dung.

The next time you cross swords with an elderly paleontologist you'll be glad to have this word in your verbal quiver.

coprolith /KOP ruh lith/ n ❧ A hardened ball of excrement.

"At majestic Stoolhenge, one can gasp in awe at the massive **coprolith** monuments of a lost civilization."

coprophagous /ko PROF uh gus/ adj ❧ Dung-eating.

A person who eats dung is a **coprophagist**.

"Billy, the **coprophagous** circus dwarf, was always a big hit with the crowds, gamely trotting along in the wake of the

trained ponies and disposing of what they left behind in his own special way—and always with a smile and a flourish."
syn **merdivorous, rhypophagous, scatophagous, stercovorous**

coprophiliac /*ko pro FILL ee ak*/ n ❧ A sexual deviant with an abnormal interest in feces.

Another word that, while perfectly offensive and usable in its own right, can also easily be used in a figurative sense.

"The politician gave a speech that night which many insiders considered to be the best of his career, in which he derided the press as 'nothing more than a bunch of bloodsucking **coprophiliacs**.' "
compare **coprolagnia**

cotquean /*KOT kween*/ n ❧ A man who involves himself overmuch in women's affairs; used disparagingly.

Cotquean is Anglo-Saxon for "house woman": *cot* (small house) + *quean* (woman). It owes its sting as a term of derision to the entrenched belief that men and women have their proper respective roles; as this belief comes under attack, the word loses some bite. Even so, we shall probably never see the day when men assume the mantle of **cotquean** with pride.

crapulent /*KRAP yoo lent*/ adj ❧ Sick from drinking and/or eating too much.

Crapulent sounds so perfect for what it describes that it's hard to believe it has no connection whatsoever with *crap* or *crappy*. But it is an unrelated word with a long history, derived from the Latin *crapula* (Greek *kraipale*), meaning "drunken sickness."

compare **bilious**

cremaster /krem ASS ter/ n · One of the muscles responsible for pulling the testicles up toward the body, as in response to cold.

"With thorough and conscientious practice, Laughton had advanced from a mere dabbling in Eastern meditation all the way to **cremaster** exercises involving fishing weights."

compare **shram**

cresty /KRESS tee/ adj · Afflicted with piles (hemorrhoids).

Have you heard of people accidentally brushing their teeth with hemorrhoid ointment? It's been known to happen, but just think how much more frequently this tragic mishap would occur if there were a brand called **Cresty**.

"After his checkup, Winthorpe felt like crying: Would he have to go through life not just short, fat, and bald, but **cresty** as well?"

cuckquean /KUK kween/ n · A female cuckold; a woman whose husband is unfaithful.

Not as well-known as *cuckold,* perhaps because a woman with a cheating husband has traditionally been an object more of sympathy than scorn. It behooves us to dust off **cuckquean** and attack this blatant double standard.

compare **wittol**

curpin /KUR pin/ n ❧ The ass of a chicken or some other fowl.

"As she watched Kenneth greedily devour his meal of fried **curpin** in hot garlic sauce, Cynthia made a silent promise to herself that this, their first date, would also be their last."

cyesolagnia /sigh ESS o LAG nee uh/ n ❧ The lust for pregnant women.

Proof that man is the most depraved animal in the world, for **cyesolagnia** makes no evolutionary sense at all. If there were a gene for it, wouldn't it have died out long ago? How could it be passed down, if **cyesolagniacs** waste their reproductive energy chasing after women who are already pregnant?

"Despite his family's worsening poverty, Gabriel shunned contraception, not because he wanted more children, but because of his closet **cyesolagnia.**"

cypripareunia /sip rip uh ROO nee uh/ n ❧ Sex with a prostitute.

"Gomez knew that Mona in Accounting didn't own a dictionary, so he went ahead and included an entry for **cypripareunia** on his expense sheet."

compare **philopornist**

·D·

dasypygal /*dass ip EYE gull*/ adj ❧ Hairy-assed.

"Dr. Plimpton's heart sank when he entered his bedroom and found his attractive young wife being mounted by Ramon, the **dasypygal** gardener."

dehorner /*dee HORN er*/ n ❧ A rubbing alcohol addict.

This gem comes to us via the legal profession.

"Precisely because the congressman had subsequently committed suicide, David viewed exposing the man as a bulemic **dehorner** to be the crown jewel of his journalistic career."

dejector /*dee JEK tor*/ n ❧ A drastic medicine for constipation.

"What Mrs. Ruskin didn't know was that France's quince chutney was, in fact, a **dejector** of unparalled potency—otherwise she might not have had a third helping before rushing to the airport to climb aboard the plane to Moscow."

compare **obstipation**

dysania /diss AY nee uh/ n ❧ Difficulty getting out of bed in the morning.

There are many words in these pages that are great to use when calling in sick to work. Of these, **dysania** is the absolute best.

"I'm so sorry to miss the all-day meeting, but I'm afraid I've come down with a bad case of **dysania**." Few bosses would be cruel—or well read—enough to reject such a plaint for mercy.

compare **matutolagnia, ergophobia**

dyscallignia /diss kuh LIG nee uh/ n ❧ The dislike of beautiful women.

A disease that primarily afflicts women who are less than beautiful.

dyschezia /diss KEE zee uh/ n ❧ Loss of the normal reflex to void the rectum, due to irregular practices.

If you're wondering what "irregular practices" are, you probably should just move on.

❧ E ❧

ecdemolagnia /ek dem o LAG nee uh/ n ❧ Extreme lustfulness when one is away from home.

Otherwise known as "marriage."

compare **uxoravalent**

edeomania /ed ee o MAY nee uh/ n ❧ An obsession with genitals.

"We all enjoyed visiting the Jurgen family, especially at Christmastime, but it might have been even more enjoyable if their several large dogs hadn't been quite so **edeomaniacal** with their snouts."

compare **lecheur**

effluvium /eh FLOO vee um/ n ❧ A slight or unseen noxious vapor.

A classy word. Integral to the motto of the Wind Breaker's Club: E Pluribus **Effluvium** (Out of Many, Smelly Gas).

"Uncomfortably, the guests quietly coughed and eyed one another strangely; no one ever discovered that the subtle **effluvium** that came and went all evening had actually been the secret contribution of Snowball, the pet Persian."

elaterium /el uh TEER ee um/ n ❧ The juice of the Squirting Cucumber.

A little clarification: The Squirting Cucumber (*Ecballium elaterium*) is an actual plant of the gourd family, the juice of which yields a drastic purgative.

If for reasons of delicacy you have need of an obscure metaphor, **elaterium** is the word for you.

"Nadia adored the tenderness with which her botany professor made love, but found it irritating when he trumpeted 'Hold me fast, dear! My **elaterium** bursts forth!'"

compare **dejector**

elumbated /el UM bay ted/ adj ❧ Weak in the loins.

This word describes the unhappy state of certain older men who take much younger wives and subsequently become **elumbated** from the constant pressure to perform in bed. Typical symptoms include: dark, liverish circles under the eyes, the paying of undue attention to diet and exercise, and the spending of hour upon hour desperately combing through Chinatown apothecaries in search of vitalizing herbal tonics.

"Dewey cursed himself for his incessant and chronic masturbation: offered a chance to score with a real-live girl, he'd been far too **elumbated** to perform."

compare **pudendagra**

encopresis /*EN ko PREE sis*/ n 🐦 Inability to control the bowels.

Here is a word that literally means to lose one's shit. Best used in sentences like the following:

"Mr. and Mrs. Spatchcock nearly had **encopresis** when they returned from their trip abroad and found that a troupe of carrot-farming squatters had laid claim to their lawn."

syn copracrasia

enuresis /*en yoo REE sis*/ n 🐦 Bed-wetting.

"Jefferey's parents just couldn't bring themselves to wean their little darling off diapers at a respectable age—leaving him with a lifelong case of **enuresis**."

compare nocturia

ephemeromorph /*ef EM er o morf*/ n 🐦 Term used to describe the lowest forms of life imaginable, so low they cannot be otherwise classified.

Evade classification though they might, **ephemeromorphs** can easily be recognized. They are usually seen blocking intersections in their cars, or, in the subway, clipping their nails while taking up three seats.

epigynum /*ep ih JINE um*/ n 🐦 The vagina of a spider.

"With the prospect of **epigynum** luring him forward, Max, the black widow, ignored the obvious danger and advanced into the web."

ergophobia /ERG o FO bee uh/ n ∿ Hatred or fear of work.

Because phobias are boring, dime-a-dozen affairs, only two are included in this book. **Ergophobia** is one of them. A word so useful should be brought to people's attention, phobia though it may be.

compare **dysania**

erotomania /eh ROTE o MAY nee uh/ n ∿ Obsessive, uncontrollable craving for sex.

"Jacobson's **erotomania** had led him down many dark and dangerous paths before, but now, as he faced the mob of enraged harpies, he realized for the first time that he needed help."

syn **lascivia, tentigo**
compare **satyriasis**

eructation /eh ruk TAY shun/ n ∿ A belching; also, the gas brought up by belching.

"Allan picked up the telephone reciever and winced; a waft of the last person's **eructations** still lingered in the mouthpiece."

compare **fumosities, nidorosities**

eviration /eh vir AY shun/ n ∿ Effeminization; the assumption of female mannerisms by a man.

"It certainly was disconcerting to see a big, strong lumberjack like Rusty undergo a complete **eviration** in the infirmary, all because of one little splinter."

excerebrose /*ex SEH reh brose*/ adj ❧ Having no brain. A smart-ass way to say *stupid*.
>   compare **witling**

expeditate /*ex PED it ate*/ v ❧ To hobble a dog by cutting out the balls of its feet.
Formerly practiced to keep dogs from chasing deer.
>   syn **hamble**

F

fadge /FAJ/ n ❧ A clumsy oaf.

"From the vantage point of a comfortable middle age, Mr. Johnstone looked back fondly on his public-school days, especially the crisp autumn mornings when he and his mates would torture and humiliate the class **fadge**, often reducing the poor boy to tears."

feague /FEEG/ v ❧ To insert an energizing suppository into the anus of a horse, in order to make it sprightly and to perk up its tail.

Feague has had a wide variety of meanings over the centuries, from "a dull, lazy oaf" to "to whip or thrash someone." The only definition that interests us, however, concerns the anus of a horse.

In times gone by, **feaguing** was commonly employed to "pep up" horses being shown for sale. A good **feague** could consist of one of several things, the most common being a suppository of raw ginger. In a pinch (or if stronger measures were called for, as in the case of a par-

❧ Feague ❧

ticularly sluggish or decrepit nag), owners sometimes resorted to the insertion of a live eel.

It is hard to imagine a less enviable job than that of *feaguer*.

Interestingly, **feague** was at one time used in a figurative sense, to mean to encourage or lift the spirits of a person.

compare **trocar**

fecaloid /*FEEK uh loid*/ adj ❧ Resembling dung.

Now, instead of expressing your displeasure by calling something shitty, or saying that it looks, smells, or sounds like shit, you may damn it as **fecaloid**.

"And so off we went, to yet another blistering Fourth

of July picnic, where I would be obliged to eat several of my father-in-law's burnt and **fecaloid** hamburgers while enduring his inane chatter."

syn **ordurous, stercoraceous**
compare **urinous**

fenks /FENX/ n, pl 🐌 Discarded whale blubber, once used for manuring.

"The docks were often a dangerous place for a land-lubber, so scattered were they with slippery **fenks**."

compare **flense**

ferule /FEH rull/ v 🐌 To punish schoolchildren by striking them on the hands with a **ferule** (a short stick or ruler).

"Mr. Peabody, the headmaster, had always been a zealous advocate of the **ferule**; after the school ended its use, he quietly took to drink."

syn **pandy**
compare **bastinado**

fimiculous /fim IK yoo luss/ adj 🐌 Dwelling in dung; existing on excrement.

"Sleeping in the barn was a step up in life for Gruber, the **fimiculous** manure boy."

compare **shardborn**

flagellant /FLAJ uh lent/ n 🐌 A sexual deviant who enjoys beating or being beaten.

49

❧ *Flagellant* ❧

"A serious **flagellant,** Rufus would twice weekly immerse his entire body in a tub of cold cream in order to render himself all the more sensitive to the delicious taste of the whip."

compare **algolagnia**

flatus /*FLAT us*/ n ❧ Gas in the stomach or intestines. Also, gas expelled from the anus.

This word, from the Latin for "a blowing," is one technical term for a fart.

compare **bdolotic, carminative, meteorism**

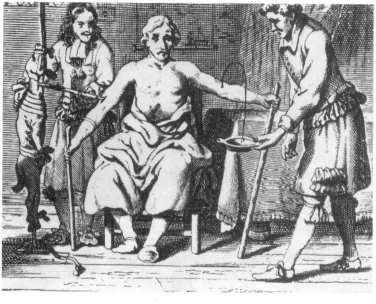

❧ *Fleam* ❧

fleam /FLEEM/ n ❧ A hollow lancet formerly used by surgeons to pierce the flesh and draw blood.

"Maybe it was just too far ahead of its time, but Doctor Barber's **fleam**-exchange program never quite caught on."

compare **bdellatomy**

flense /FLENZ/ v ❧ To strip the blubber off an animal such as a whale.

"Diets were useless, exercise out of the question: nothing outside of a drastic **flensing** could help Otto, the human medicine ball."

compare fenks

franion /FRAN yun/ n ❧ A man of loose behavior; a pleasure seeker.

It is one of the gross inequalities of the English language that while there are literally dozens of words to describe women of promiscuous behavior, words for their male counterparts are exceedingly scarce. So make the most of **franion**.

compare cicisbeo

fricatrice /FRIK uh triss/ n ❧ A harlot; a lewd woman. Also, a lesbian; a female genital rubber.

Were it not for its secondary meaning, **fricatrice,** like countless other English words for women of dubious morals—including (to name a few) *gig, giglet, callet, cocotte, blowen, drassock, dratchel, drotchel, drazel, doxy, cyprian, paphian, leman, leveret, mab, puttock, rep, demirep, slattern, slaister, ploot, jade, demimondaine, meretrix, harlot, strumpet,* and *quean*—would not have made it into this book.

compare tribade

frottage /FROT ij/ n ❧ The practice of rubbing up against another person while clothed, in the pursuit of sexual satisfaction.

Isn't it comforting to know that the next time you're on a city bus and someone presses his groin against your butt, you will have a word for it?

frotteur /fro TIRRH/ n 🐦 A man who performs **frottage**. A female **frotteur** is known as a *frotteuse*.

fubsy /FUB zee/ adj 🐦 Plump and squat.
There are many, many words to describe short and fat people in the English language. Most of them, for reasons that remain unclear, are of Scottish origin, and the overwhelming majority of them are very dull indeed. Since it is unlikely that you will ever come across the need for more than one of these words, the authors give you **fubsy**.

"Behind six months in his rent, Nestor heard the pounding at his door and ran to the back exit, only to be intercepted by his **fubsy**, rolling-pin-wielding landlady."
compare **smatchet**

fumosities /few MOSS it eez/ n 🐦 Ill-smelling vapors from a drunken person's belches.
" 'How did you know the defendant was under the influence?' the judge asked the testifying officer. 'I smelled his **fumosities**, sir,' he replied."
compare **eructation, nidorosities**

Fussock

fussock */FUSS uk/* n ~ A large, fat woman.

A good word to use, for instance, for the lady ahead of you in line who accidentally stomps on your foot with her ridiculously tiny heels.

"Eventually Wilbur's passion overcame him, and he plunged into the **fussock** like a squirrel into a pile of leaves."

compare **fustilugs**

~ *Fustigate* ~

fustigate */FUSS tig ate/* v ~ To beat with a stick or club.

A hearty, meaty word. Sometimes it is a good idea to

relax, sit back, and think of all the people you would like to see **fustigated**. From the Latin *fustis* (club), *fustuarium* (execution by clubbing), and *fustigare* (to cudgel to death).

fustilugs /*FUSS tee lugs*/ n ❧ An unwieldy and slovenly woman.

"Life as a circus fat lady was no walk in the park, Edelle the **fustilugs** realized. Despite her immense girth, she was expected to trot around the entire ring thrice daily."

compare **fussock**

G

gambrinous /*GAM brin us*/ adj ❧ Full of beer.

"Helmut was never able to leave a soiree until he was properly **gambrinous,** and usually suffered horribly the next morning as a result."

compare potvaliant

gamomania /*gam o MAY nee uh*/ n ❧ Insanity characterized by the compulsion to make outlandish marriage proposals.

"In order to avoid an extremely expensive settlement with his estranged wife, Benson embraced an unusual legal strategy: annullment by reason of **gamomania.**"

ganch /*GANCH*/ v ❧ To execute by impaling upon hooks or stakes.

Victims of this delightful practice were often tossed from a platform onto the aforementioned hooks and stakes. Even today, careless casting can result in bystanders being **ganched** on the fishing pier.

"After an exquisite meal, guests retired to the salon for

snifters of cognác, where Bishop Montleby's suggestion that **ganching** be reinstated for debtors was met with hearty approval from all assembled."

gardyloo /gar dee LOO/ exclamation ❧ Formerly, a cry given just prior to throwing household slops or the contents of one's chamber pot out the window, warning those on the street below.

gavage /guv AHZH/ n ❧ The force-feeding of geese or other fowl to fatten them or enlarge their livers. Also, any force-feeding.

" 'What goes around comes around,' thought Wendy at Christmas dinner, as her grandmother piled more of the burnt goose—probably a victim of **gavage** itself—onto her plate."

compare **impinguinate**

genicon /JEN ik on/ n ❧ An imagined sexual partner visualized during sex, in order to facilitate pleasure.

(The imagined partner can be real, just not present at the time.)

"Sonya eventually grew tired of trying to force herself to be attracted to her husband, and relied more and more upon her **genicons** for fulfillment."

geromorphism /jeh ro MORF ism/ n ❧ The condition of appearing older than one's age.

"In a state of total denial, Penny refused to even consider that her daily tanning sessions might have something to do with her advanced **geromorphism**."

gerontophilia /*jeh ront uh FEEL ee uh*/ n ❧ Sexual attraction to elderly men.

"No lecher was he—merely another victim of the latest sexual fad of bored and hip young women: **gerontophilia**."
compare **anililagnia**

giddhom /*GID hum*/ n ❧ The frantic galloping of cows plagued by flies.

Giddhom is such an amusing and potentially useful word—why not extend its meaning to cover, say, human beings on camping trips?

"Three nights and two days of hell and Dylan snapped; unfortunately, his half-mad **giddhom** only had the effect of attracting thicker clouds of mosquitoes."

gleet /*GLEET*/ n ❧ In ascending order of vileness:

1. any slimy and viscous substance
2. a persistent sinus inflammation
3. a thick phlegm found in the stomachs of hawks
4. thin, milky urethral discharge
5. runoff from a gonorrheal sore

gobbets /*GOB its*/ n, pl ❧ Pieces of human bodies that wash ashore from a shipwreck.

Gobbet, a generic word for a lump of flesh, is more familiar to most people than **gobbets**, which is remarkable for its gruesome specificity.

compare **adipocere**

gound /*GOWND*/ n ➤ The crusty yellow substance that collects in the corners of one's eyes while one sleeps.

Everybody gets this stuff in the corners of their eyes while they sleep, and nobody really knows what to call it. Typical terms invented to fill this vacuum include sleepies, eye-snot, and bed-boogers. The correct word, however, is gound.

"Collin was never one to dilly dally in the morning: by the time he had rubbed the **gound** out of his eyes he was usually on his third Manhattan."

graveolent /*gruh VAY o lent*/ adj ➤ Having an offensive and fetid odor.

There are so many horrible smells in the world. In fact, fifty new ones are invented every day. New words to describe them, therefore, should be welcomed by all.

groak /*GROAK*/ v ➤ To stare silently at someone while they are eating, in the hope that they will offer some food.

Groak is one of the finest all-around words in this book. It is fun to say, easy to remember, and somehow manages to sound like what it means, even though what it describes is a silent action. And the definition, while not as depraved as some other words, is both amusing and instantly applicable in life.

"Flowers, reservations for two at the best restaurant in town: Trevor's date was going exactly as planned—except for the pair of **groaking** hobos with their noses pressed right up against the glass."

compare scrambler

gugusse /guh GOOSE/ n ꙮ A young homosexual with a penchant for priests.

"The cardinal sought out a plump young **gugusse** for himself, but had to settle for a slightly unwilling altar-boy."

compare gunsel

gunsel /GUN zul/ n ꙮ The orally passive member of a male homosexual union. Also, a gunman.

A word with an unusual history. It entered the English language from the German *gänslein* (little goose) and originally meant a passive male lover. But in 1929, Dashiell Hamett slyly inserted it into his famous novel *The Maltese Falcon* in reference to a young homosexual gunman. Since many people at the time seemed ignorant of the fact that two men could be lovers, **gunsel** was read by most as a simple synonym for "gunman". This secondary meaning has since remained in the language.

compare gugusse, irrumate

gurry /*GIRRH ee*/ n ✦ Medical waste from dissecting rooms. Also, refuse from fishing and whaling.

"Chip knew it was a demanding way to work his way through medical school, but bagging up the **gurry** happened to be one of the highest-paying jobs on campus."

compare **fenks**

gynander /*guy NAN der*/ n ✦ A mannish woman.

"In a last-ditch effort to elude his homosexual tendencies, Cromwell married a young **gynander** who came equipped with both a vile temper and a significant moustache."

compare **viraginity**

gynecomast /*GUY nek o mast*/ n ✦ A man suffering from **gynecomastia** (outsized, flaccid, feminine breasts).

gynecomastia /*guy nek o MAST ee uh*/ n ✦ A condition whereby a man's breasts swell to abnormal size, coming to resemble those of a woman in appearance and/or function.

"A shortage of nondairy creamer threatened to disrupt the third annual **Gynecomastia** Society luncheon, but the crisis was soon averted."

gynopiper /*GUY no pipe er*/ n ✦ One who stares lewdly at women.

One of the beautiful things about **gynopiper** is that, like its cousin **arrhenopiper**, it does not specify the sex of the person doing the ogling.

compare **arrhenopiper**

H

hamble /HAM bull/ v ❧ To cripple a dog by cutting out the balls of its feet.

"Jefferson, the unbalanced mailman, finally snapped one day: his arrest for criminal assault with intent to **hamble** a cocker spaniel made the evening news."

syn **expeditate**

hamesucken /HAME suk en/ n ❧ Felonious assault of someone in his own home.

Go on, laugh! It's *funny!*

hemothymia /hee mo THIGH mee uh/ n ❧ The irresistable desire to murder.

"When her husband announced that he was leaving her for a woman named Kiki twenty years her junior, Doris felt the **hemothymia** begin to swell within her."

hircine /HER sine/ adj ❧ Smelling like a goat.

"Had he been a tad less **hircine**, I might actually have

enjoyed my afternoon sessions with the venerable Monsignor Wilby."

syn **caprylic**

compare **rammish**

hircismus /*her SIZ muss*/ n ❧ A malodorous condition of the armpits.

"So worried was Prufrock about his **hircismus** that prior to his big date he wrapped his armpits entirely with duct tape."

compare **maschalephidrosis**

❧ *Hemothymia* ❧

huskanoy /*HUSK uh noy*/ v ∿ To subject to repeated enemas, especially as a form of initiation.

"At the press conference, the dean emphatically defended the fraternities that had come under fire for hazing: 'So what if a few of the lads have been getting **huskanoyed** here and there,' he said, 'where's the harm in that?' "

compare **clyster**

hypereccrisia /*hi per ek RIZH ee uh*/ n ∿ An abnormal amount of excretion.

If the sheer quantity of what lies in the bowl defies the senses and makes you worry about the capacity of your household plumbing, then you are truly suffering from **hypereccrisia**.

"When her little brother yelled from the bathroom for her to 'come quick,' Flo replied with disgust that she had absolutely no desire to bear witness to his **hypereccrisia**."

hyperemesis /*hi per EM eh sis*/ n ∿ Abnormally profuse or prolonged vomiting.

"If only someone had warned Mary of the in-laws' cat's chronic **hyperemesis,** she would never have sported with it in such a rough-and-tumble fashion, and might have been spared the indignity of sitting through dinner with her husband's family while clad in a borrowed housedress several sizes too big."

compare **bespew, vomiturition**

hypergenitalism /hi per JEN it ull ism/ n ✎ Over-development of the genitals.

"Osgood's **hypergenitalism** did not pass unnoticed by the talent scouts at the annual "Please, Make Me a Star"convention in Pasadena."

compare **macrogenitosomia, macrophallus, mentulate**

hypogenitalism /hi po JEN it ull ism/ n ✎ Stunted growth of the genitals.

"Little Chucky Stead had a hard life: the unrelenting acne, the layer of baby fat that just wouldn't go away, and worst of all, the severe **hypogenitalism** for which there was no remedy . . , would things ever get better?"

syn **microgenitalism**

hypomazia /hi po MAY zee uh/ n ✎ Underdevelopment of the breasts.

Lest the reader misinterpret the tone of this book, the authors offer the following clarification: We have nothing against small breasts. We have nothing against large breasts, or breasts of any kind.

syn **micromastia**
compare **macromastia**

I

iatronudia /*eye at ro NOO dee uh*/ n ❧ A woman's pretending to be ill out of a desire to disrobe in front of a doctor.

"There was something fishy here: after the young lady stripped naked to 'show him her hangnail,' Doctor Willoughby began to suspect he had a case of **iatronudia** on his hands."

compare **apodyopsis**

igly /*IG lee*/ adj ❧ Extremely ugly.

Essentially, something qualifies as **igly** when it is uglier than ugly.

illitate /*ILL it ate*/ v ❧ To overdecorate the female face.

Not to be confused with *irritate,* even though **illitating** might indeed irritate friends, husbands, or anybody with good taste.

immerd /*im URD*/ v ❧ To cover with excrement.

"No one claimed responsibility for **immerding** the supervisor's car, but suspicion immediately fell on Morgan, who was seen consuming copious quantities of coffee and pork rinds in the hours before the incident."

syn beray, bescumber, conskite
compare ordurous, sharny, shitten

imparlibidinous /IM par lib ID in us/ adj ～ Pertaining to an unequal state of desire between two people

A word that gloriously and succinctly describes a state of affairs we all know far too well. When you ask the woman of your dreams out on a date and she laughs, spits on you, and says she would rather couple with a rhino, simply explain to your friends that the two of you were imparlibidinous.

impinguinate /im PING win ate/ v ～ To fatten.

"A jealous woman by nature, Yvette would cook an impinguinating dinner for her husband every night in the hope of making him less desirable to other women."

compare bariatrics, gavage

infibulate /in FIB yoo late/ v ～ To practice infibulation upon: to fit with a chastity belt or otherwise tie down, lock up, or sew shut a person's genitals to prevent him or her from having sex.

A word that might, for instance, be applied to that poor sap in college who, with his weasely face, flaccid

❧ *Infibulate* ❧

physique, and chronic nasal drip, might as well have been
infibulated for all the chance he had of getting laid.

"His political star had risen quickly among his conser-
vative constituents, due in large measure to his calling for
the **infibulation** of the state's many welfare recipients."

initiatrix */in ish ee AY trix/* n ❧ A female initiator.
A rather broad definition that lends itself to a specific
and salacious inference.

"Charlie got a lot of money at his bar mitzvah, but the best present didn't come in an envelope at all: his older brother took him to an **initiatrix** on the other side of town."

intromission /in tro MISH un/ n ❧ Insertion of the penis into the vagina.

At the theater, if they announced that there would be a short **intromission** between the acts, a good percentage of the audience might remain in their seats instead of ducking outside for a smoke.

"It was precisely at the moment of **intromission** that Bixby remembered he had neglected to turn off the coffee maker at work—things went downhill from there."

irrumate /ih roo MATE/ v ❧ To insert one's penis into someone's mouth.

irrumation /ih roo MAY shun/ n ❧ The act of **irrumating** (see above).

"He was a kind and sweet man, and their love affair would have lasted longer had he not been so brutishly persistent in his **irrumations**."

compare **lecheur**

J

janiform /JAN if orm/ adj ❧ Two-faced.

A word unsuitable for politicians, who after all have many more than just *two* faces.

jarble /JAR bul/ v ❧ To spatter with something; wet; bemire.

"Roger cursed his unsteady hands; he had **jarbled** himself in the hotel bathroom, and now he was obliged to get up close and personal with the electric hand dryer."
compare **lantrify**

jugulate /JUG yoo late/ v ❧ To throttle or cut the throat of; attack by the neck; hang by the neck.

Finally, a word that covers any kind of neck attack. Talk about useful—however did we get by without **jugulate**?

jumentous /joo MENT us/ adj ❧ Smelling like horse urine. Also, resembling horse urine in color and frothiness.

This delightful word is a wolf in sheep's clothing: it

sounds festive and jolly, but actually has a stinking, disgusting meaning. That makes it perfect for undetectable insults: "This haggis is just **jumentous**," you might say, or "a **jumentous** time was had by all," or "I'd like to thank all of you for joining us on this most **jumentous** occasion."

Janiform

K

kakidrosis /kak id RO sis/ n ❧ The secretion of foul-smelling perspiration.

"Although the ammonia carried with it a certain sting, Bruce found that nothing else could dampen his **kakidrosis**."

syn **bromidrosis**
compare **podobromhidrosis**

keck /KEK/ v ❧ To attempt to vomit without success.

Even more onomatopoeic than the familiar, almost-synonomous *retch*.

"When the exact nature of the dumplings we had just eaten was made known to us there was a mad stampede for the bathroom, but alas, we could do no more than **keck**."

compare **vomiturition**

keech /KEECH/ n ❧ A lump of rolled-up fat.

A small and ugly word.

compare **fenks**

kleptolagnia /klept o LAG nee uh/n 🦢 Sexual excitement from stealing.

"Oswald's thievery grew to keep pace with his insatiable **kleptolagnia,** until he began taking risks that culminated in his ignoble and acutely embarrassing apprehension."

kordax /KORE dax/ n ● A penis dance performed by horned figures in the Dionysian festivals of ancient Greece.

"The PTA at our high school was dead set against having the students organize their own dance; to them, anything less sedate than foxtrot night might as well have been a **kordax**."

lairwite /*LAIR white*/ n ❧ A fine formerly levied for adultery.

"Not only did Trevor have to pay the **lairwite** as a result of his transgressions, but his wife dumped boiling water on his lap."

compare **lenocinium**

lant /*LANT*/ n ❧ Stale urine used in manufacturing.

That's right: manufacturing. What kind? Wool-scouring, for one. Happy?

"The labor dispute at the textile plant got really ugly after union workers began dunking their supervisors in the **lant** vat."

compare **lotium**

lantrify /*LANT rif eye*/ v ❧ To moisten with urine.

A unique and mystifying word. How many things are there that get moistened with urine routinely enough to have necessitated a term for this action? With luck, we shall never know.

"The cookbook had to be recalled when it was discovered that the recipe for chutney quiche on page 84 called for the **lantrifying** of the crust prior to baking. (It was, after all, supposed to be a *vegetarian* cookbook.)"

lapidable /LAP id uh bul/ adj ∿ Worthy of being stoned.

If you are prevented by courtesy from expressing what you really think of the meal, simply say "The chef is really quite **lapidable**."

lapidate /LAP id ate/ v ∿ To stone; to kill by hurling rocks at.

"After Mike ran over the headman's favorite goat while stoned on hashish, it began to look like he would be **lapidated** by irate villagers."

compare fustigate

lascivia /luh SIV ee uh/ n ∿ Abnormally strong sexual desire.

Lascivia, then, is the condition of inordinate *lasciviousness*.

"Pomerantz's **lascivia** served him in good stead; when it was discovered, he was passed over for the eunuchs and placed instead in the queen's retinue."

syn erotomania, tentigo
compare satyriasis

lask /LASK/ v ∿ To be afflicted with diarrhea.

Lenocinium

" 'I'm sorry,' said the secretary, 'but Mr. Cooper happens to be **lasking** at the moment. May I take a message?' "

compare collywobbles

lecheur /lay SHIRRH/ n ❧ A licker of genitals.

"Weights, yoga, intricate furniture arrangements—Peabody tried everything as part of his all-consuming ambition to be an auto-**lecheur**."

compare irrumation

lenocinium /len o SIN ee um/ n ❧ Accepting or encouraging infidelity in one's wife in return for monetary gain.

"The other men in the village might jeer him, but in the last year alone Walter had purchased a new cart, a slightly-used plow, and several fine young hogs—and **lenocinium** had paid for it all."

compare wittol

lientery /LIE en teh ree/ n ❧ Diarrhea consisting of undigested or semidigested food.

"Howie's **lientery** might not have been quite so uncomfortable had he not consumed three jars of pigs' feet the night before."

compare chyme

lobcock /LOB cock/ n ❧ A stupid, clumsy person.

" 'You stupid, clumsy man,' cried the vicar's wife after Maynard broke his third piece of china, 'why, you're nothing but a **lobcock**!' "

❧ *Lotium* ❧

lotium /LO shum/ n ☙ Stale urine formerly used by barbers as a cosmetic for the hair.

Lotium is Latin for urine.

"Imagine Allison's profound unease when she discovered her roommate had been spiking the house shampoo with her own homemade **lotium**."

compare **lant**

lovertine /LUV er teen/ adj ☙ Addicted to sex.

Describing someone as **lovertine** sounds so much more poetic than calling them a raving sex maniac, doesn't it?

compare **philopornist**

· M ·

macrogaster /MAK ro gas ter/ n ❧ A person with a big belly.

One of the ironies of today is that so many of those who freely dispense pompous bits of advice on how to eat healthily are **macrogasters** themselves.

"Drawing inspiration from such eclectic sources as hospital maternity gowns and butcher's smocks, Flavian made a killing with a line of clothes specifically designed for the hip young **macrogasters** of today."

macrogenitosomia /MAK ro jen it o SO mee uh/ n ❧ Oversized penis in a newborn.

Blessing or curse? You decide.

"To their collective revulsion, the nurses in the maternity ward realized that the extra swagger in the step of the vile and loathsome Mr. Perkins was actually a reaction to his newborn son's **macrogenitosomia**."

macromastia /MAK ro MAST ee uh/ n ❧ The development of abnormally large breasts.

Macrogaster

"It was as the surgeon explained to her that the implants came in three sizes—Large, Extra Large, and **Macromastia**—that Jill first began to have her doubts about the operation."

compare **bathycolpian, mammose**

macrophallus */mak ro FAL us/* n ❧ An inordinately large penis.

"While he knew his was no **macrophallus,** Montgomery had always hoped that in the dark no one would be the wiser."

compare **byental, mentulate, microphallus**

mageira /*muh JY ruh*/ n ✎ A woman's sublimation of sexual desire through cooking.

"Sex was okay, but what Marty really liked was eating, and to this end he fostered his wife's **mageira** by making love to her as infrequently as possible."

mammose /*mam OSE*/ adj ✎ Having an ample bosom.

A perfectly serviceable little word for massive melons.

" 'Were Madame not quite so . . . **mammose**,' said Victor the tailor tactfully, 'a size three would certainly have been *plausible* . . . ' "

compare **bathycolpian, macromastia**

mammothrept /*MAM o thrept*/ n ✎ A spoiled child.

From the Greek *mammothreptos* (a child raised by its grandmother).

"Dr. Luetic's revolutionary book on child rearing, *Subdue Your Kid!* became a runaway best-seller when word got out that he recommended the severe paddling of **mammothrepts**."

compare **misopedia**

maritodespotism /*mar it o DESS pot ism*/ n ✎ Ruthless domination of a wife by her husband.

"Ned's attempts to usher in a new era of **maritodespotism** to his marriage backfired badly, as his wife—who had previously ignored him—now began to beat him regularly."

maschalephidrosis /*mass kuh lef id RO sis*/ n ☙ Runaway armpit perspiration.

"Although the woman at the pharmacy looked at him oddly when he bought multiple boxes of superabsorbent panty liners, Hugo had found that nothing less could handle the task of mopping up his **maschalephidrosis**."
compare **bromidrosis, podobromhidrosis, hircismus**

mastigophoric /*mass tig o FOR ik*/ adj ☙ Whip-wielding.

"The Duchovnys were a rather eccentric couple, as could be inferred from the blown-up photo of a leering Mrs. Duchovny, *in delicato* and **mastigophoric**, dominating the dining room."
compare **algolagnia**

mastoptosis /*mass TOE TOE sis*/ n ☙ Sagging, pendulous breasts.

"Liza's boyfriend liked her **mastoptosis**; she, on the other hand, found letting out all her bras an enormous hassle."
compare **mazopexy**

matutolagnia /*may too toe LAG nee uh*/ n ☙ The desire to have sex in the morning.

"After his wife's **matutolagnia** made him miss his fourth consecutive morning meeting, George started looking for work as a night watchman."
compare **dysania**

mazopexy /*MAZE o pex ee*/ n ❧ Surgery to lift sagging breasts.

"His business was listed under 'Body Enhancements,' but the Hollywood cognoscenti knew him as the **mazopexist** to the stars."

compare **mastoptosis**

mazophilous /*maze o FIL us*/ adj ❧ Fond of breasts.

"His friends all thought that Humphrey was too overtly **mazophilous,** and they were secretly amused when he had all of his fingers viciously broken after he proved it with the wrong woman."

compare **pygophilous**

meable /*MEE uh bull*/ adj ❧ Easily penetrated.

Meable does not have an overtly sexual definition, but lends itself so perfectly to innuendo that the distinction is moot. Use this word as you see fit; we hope you'll have many an opportunity to do so.

meconium /*meh KONE ee um*/ n ❧ A baby's first feces after being born; a dark green tarlike excretion containing mucus, bile, and shed cells.

None of the medical literature consulted addresses the central question: Does it stink, or does that come later?

compare **steatorrhea**

megarectum /MEG uh REK tum/ n ❧ A rectum that is overly dilated.

"Proud possessor of a **megarectum,** Alphonse put it to lucrative use in such underground cinema classics as *Chambre à Louer* (Room to Spare) and *Chatouille-Moi à L'Intérieur* (Tickle Me Inside)."

meldrop /MEL drop/ n ❧ A drop of liquid suspended at the end of the nose.

"He was one of those sad and undersized schoolboys, always with a **meldrop** that he would periodically wipe on his sleeve."

mentulate /MENT yoo late/ adj ❧ Possessing a large penis.

"Being **mentulate** wasn't always everything it was cracked up to be, mused Barney; indeed, it was often the height of inconvenience."

compare **macrophallus**

merdivore /MURD iv or/ n ❧ An eater of excrement.

In English we have many words that relate to the eating of shit, and guess what? We need every damn one of them.

"We were all a bit put off when our host—after an admittedly delicious stew—began extolling the virtues of a **merdivorous** diet: 'Why look at those fellows, the dung beetles,' he said, 'strong as oxen, they are!' "

syn **coprophagist, scatophage**

merdurinous /*murd YOO rin us*/ *adj* ❧ Made up of urine and feces.

The reader may well decide to use this word in a metaphorical sense, perhaps to describe vile-tasting food of an indeterminate consistency.

compare **urinous**

merkin /*MUR kin*/ n ❧ A pussy wig; artificial hair for the female pudendum.

While it may seem that we have no real need for such an article today, at one time **merkins** were greatly in demand. On the French Can-Can stage, for example, dancers who could flash a wisp or two of pubic hair had, shall we say, a leg up on the competition. Since some women lacked the requisite hair, there arose a market for **merkins**.

"Françoise was overjoyed; after many long months of scrimping and saving, she could finally afford that luxurious new **merkin** she'd had her eye on, and throw away the cheap, itchy one that she'd bought in the thrift store on the Rue St. Denis."

metapneustic /*met uh NEW stik*/ adj ❧ Breathing through an apparatus located in the anus, as with some insects.

Metapneustic is a word that, while it is intended to describe insects, with a small stretch can also be applied to people, in particular those individuals with their heads stuck firmly up their asses.

~ *Merkin* ~

meteorism /*MEE tee or ism*/ n ❧ Bloating in the abdomen due to gas.

"After the extra buoyancy granted him by his **meteorism** saved his life in the whitewater rafting accident, Cosgrove resolved to eat as much cheese as he liked."

compare **bdolotic, carminative, flatus**

meupareunia /*moo per ROO nee uh*/ n ❧ Sexual activity in which only one partner is gratified.

"A legal precedent was set that day, as the jury agreed that Mrs. Grimthorpe's savage mutilation of her husband while he slept was indeed justified, due to her years of **meupareunia** at his hands."

compare **artamesia**

micrencephalus /*mike ren SEF uh lus*/ n 🐦 A person with an abnormally small brain.

An authoritative-sounding word to describe stupid people, such as clerks at the DMV, and insurance salesmen of any kind.

compare **excerebrose**

microgenitalism /*mike ro JEN it ul ism*/ n 🐦 A condition in which the genitals are inordinately small.

"Roland, already known to suffer from **microgenitalism** of the first order, suffered another grievous setback to his sex life with the accident on the diving board, in which he bit off the front third of his tongue."

syn **hypogenitalism**

micromania /*mike ro MAY nee uh*/ n 🐦 The delusion that a part of one's body has shrunk or is in danger of shrinking.

This is the closest word we have in English to the uniquely Chinese *koro,* the widespread hysterical conviction that one's penis is shrinking. *Koro* is recorded to have swept entire regions, driving men into such a panic that they would don protective bamboo devices before going to bed in order to guard against the disappearance of their members overnight.

compare **tarassis**

micromaniac /mike ro MAY nee ak/ n ∾ A victim of micromania; a person under the delusion that a part of his body has shrunk.

"After viewing the evidence, the judges agreed that Hannibal the **micromaniac** had definitely been the victim of a spell of belittlement. The decision was made to burn the witches."

micromastia /mike ro MASS tee uh/ n ∾ The condition of having tiny breasts.

"Some thought it inappropriate for him to advertise his breast implant practice just outside the Center for **Micromastia**, but Dr. Anderson Lee didn't care: he was rich and getting richer."

syn **amastia, hypomazia**

microphallus /mike ro FAL us/ **amastia** ∾ An abnormally small penis.

"In a pitiable effort to rectify his **microphallus,** Lewis bought a suction pump at a garage sale. The results were not encouraging."

compare **macrophallus, microgenitalism**

micturient /mik TYOO ree ent/ adj ∾ Feeling a strong desire to urinate.

The next time you are in polite company and feel the call of nature, instead of saying you have to tinkle, take a leak, or drain your hog, why not take the classy route and say you feel **micturient**?

"Being unbearably **micturient** just at the climax of the movie, Cooper thought it perfectly acceptable to relieve himself into his empty popcorn bucket; his date was less than understanding."

micturition /*mik choo RISH un*/ n ❧ Excessively frequent urination.

The Latin *mingo* (to urinate) is the root of both **micturition** and **micturient**.

syn **polakuiria**

milt /*MILT*/ n ❧ Fish semen.

Caviar is a highly esteemed delicacy—why is it that no one eats **milt?** Perhaps because the very notion is revolting.

"Pierre was a true gastronomic adventurer, but even he recoiled from the offering of **milt** on a biscuit."

misologist /*miz ALL uh jist*/ n ❧ One with a hatred of mental activity.

In these days of television, computer games, and widespread "dumbing down," the **misologists** are in the majority.

"The store manager gave Dotti an abacus when the

cash register broke down, but as a lifelong **misologist** she just couldn't be bothered trying to learn to use it."
compare **excerebrose, witling**

❧ *Misopedia* ❧

misopedia /*miz o PEE dee uh*/ n ❧ An intense, unreasonable hatred of children, especially one's own.

Misopedia does not refer to the regular, run-of-the-mill dislike we all have for the little monsters—which is, of course, normal—but only to an unusually intense and unreasonable hatred.

"As part of his revolutionary new aversion therapy for **misopedia,** Dr. Schneider would handcuff his patients to the backstop during Sunday Little League games."

compare **mammothrept**

monorchid /*mon OR kid*/ n ☙ A man with one testicle. adj ☙ Having only one testicle.

"After the badminton accident left him a **monorchid,** Mr. Spratwell flatly told his wife that their days of making love every morning and evening were over: 'I've got to conserve my fluids, dear,' he said, 'and I'm working at half-speed.' "

compare **triorchid**

mumchance /*MUM chance*/ n ☙ A silent numbskull. v ☙ To remain silent due to caution or stupidity.

"The professor had a sadistic side, and would always ferret out the **mumchances** in his class early enough to afford himself a full semester devoted to teasing and humiliating them."

compare **witling**

myatonia /*my uh TONE ee uh*/ n ☙ Flabbiness; lack of muscular fitness.

"Such was Gustave's **myatonia** that a schoolmate of his once remarked that his entire body seemed to be constructed out of ass cheeks."

compare **pyriform**

N

nanophilia /*nan o FEEL ee uh*/ n ❧ A lust for short people.

"Pasqual was crushed when his wife informed him that she could no longer combat the **nanophilia** raging in her veins, and was running off to join the much-celebrated dwarf circus."

neanilagnia /*nee AN il AG nee uh*/ n ❧ A sexual longing for young women.

"It was obvious to the kids in her sixth period gym class that Mrs. McGillucuddy suffered from more than a touch of **neanilagnia**."

compare **anililagnia, gerontophilia**

necrosadism /*nek ro SADE ism*/ n ❧ Sexual gratification from the mutilation of dead bodies.

Many people think *necrophilia* (having sex with dead people) is about as depraved as a word can possibly get—not so! **Necrosadism** ups the ante.

compare **algolagnia**

❧ *Nanophilia* ❧

nidorosity /*nide or OSS it ee*/ n ❧ A belch that tastes of cooked meat.

"Beads of perspiration began appearing on Terri's forehead, not because the waltz was tiring, but because she had to hold her breath to avoid inhaling her partner's **nidorosities**."

compare **eructation, fumosities**

nimgimmer /*NIM gim er*/ n 🐦 A physician who specializes in the treatment of venereal disease.

"After losing his license to practice medicine because of abuse of anesthesia, Lester was forced to become a back-alley **nimgimmer**."

compare **sangrado**

nisus /*NIZE us*/ n 🐦 The physical exertion involved in defecation, including the contraction of the abdominal muscles and the diaphragm. Also, the urge to mate in the spring, or any strong urge.

"It didn't matter how much oat bran and prune juice Jonathan consumed; even the most vein-popping **nisus** couldn't expel the blockage from his system."

compare **tenesmus, vernalagnia**

nocturia /*nok TYOO ree uh*/ n 🐦 Copious nocturnal urination.

"The omnipresent roar of nearby Niagara Falls may have had something to do with it, but whatever the reason, on his honeymoon Harry's **nocturia** reached a new level of inconvenience."

compare **enuresis**

nympholepsy /*NIM fo lep see*/ n 🐦 An erotic daydream trance.

A person under the spell of **nympholepsy** is known as a *nympholept*.

"Lionel was rudely awakened from his **nympholepsy** by the teacher calling him up to the blackboard to solve a lengthy algebra problem, and had to scramble to cover his excitement with a textbook."

O

obsolagnium /*ob so LAG nee um*/ n ❧ The fading of sexual desire in old age.

"Much to the shock and dismay of the young gold-digger who had married him, the ancient and hump-backed Mr. Finch showed absolutely no sign whatsoever of any **obsolagnium**."

compare **phallorhiknosis**

obstipation /*ob stip AY shun*/ n ❧ Stubborn and persistent constipation.

Just think "obstinate constipation."

"Ester was grateful for the **obstipation** she came down with on the camping trip, for she was not too keen on using leaves."

oikiomiasmata /*oy kee o mee AZ mut uh*/ n ❧ Unhealthy domestic gases; wafting pollution in a household.

The odd-looking word **oikiomiasmata** also possesses an eccentric definition: bad smells resulting from shoddy housekeeping. It comes from the combination of the Greek *oikos* (house) and *miasmata* (pollution). And it is more useful than one may think at first glance.

"Christine couldn't live with the unbearable **oikiomiasmata** any longer: although it meant losing the silent battle of wills with her brother, she decided to take out the garbage."

compare **graveolent**

ophelimity /o *fuh* LIM *it ee*/ n ❧ The ability to please one's sexual partner.

As it happens, **Ophelimity** can be wholly or partially impeded by various phenomena discussed in this book, such as **colpoxerosis** and **microphallus**.

"Where the questionnaire asked her to rate her husband's **ophelimity** on a scale of one to ten, Belinda checked 'Does Not Apply.' "

compare **anaphrodisiac**

ordured /or DURED/ adj ❧ Covered, spattered, or filled with dung.

syn **sharny, shitten**
compare **beray, bescumber, conskite, immerd**

ordurous /or DURE *us*/ adj ❧ Resembling dung; filthy.

"The kitchen staff was somewhat miffed when Mrs. Pendleton sent back the squab—haughtily referring to it as 'simply **ordurous**'—and each one of them eagerly contributed a gob of spit to her next course."

syn **fecaloid, stercoraceous**

orf /*ORF*/ n ✒ A sheep-borne skin disease that causes red, oozing sores around the mouth. No treatment is necessary; the condition eventually clears up by itself.

"Jamie wasn't about to let a little thing like a case of **orf** keep him from attending the shepherd's ball."

osphresiophilia /*oss free zee o FIL ee uh*/ n ✒ Sexual excitement from smells.

"Being a perfume tester was a dream job for a woman with **osphresiophilia,** but Nancy's frequent trips to the bathroom began to raise some eyebrows in the lab."

compare **renifleur**

ozoamblyrosis /*o zo am blih RO sis*/ n ✒ The loss of sexual desire due to the unpleasant body odor of one's partner.

"Beatrice wished that being a marriage counselor was always this easy. Immediately upon meeting Mr. Simpson she knew the problem had to be **ozoamblyrosis,** so she handed Mrs. Simpson a pair of nose plugs and spent the rest of the hour getting a pedicure."

compare **osphresiophilia**

P

pageism /*PAGE ism*/ n ❧ A mental disorder in which a man yearns to be the slave of a beautiful woman.

"Randal was a pasty man with a severe case of **pageism**, and while finding a woman willing to dominate him was easy, finding one who was also beautiful was proving to be a bit of a problem."

compare **retifism**

pandy /*PAN dee*/ v ❧ To punish someone by beating them on the hands with a stick.

"Mrs. Hedley was generally regarded as a strict disciplinarian who got results, but when she avowed the return of **pandying** for her kindergarten class the school board began to weigh her dismissal."

syn **ferule**
compare **bastinado**

paphian /*PAY fee en*/ adj ❧ Having to do with illicit love; pertaining to harlots; licentious; lewd.

"Gathered 'round the bonfire at night, the young

campers loved to listen to farmer John's tales of wily foxes and savage bears. But when he burst into tears one evening and recounted the story of his **paphian** romance with Elsa, the winsome young sheep, the children all felt a bit odd."

paracoita /para KOY tuh/ n 🕊 A female sex partner.

"Webster couldn't lie to his mother, so he told her the box at the foot of his bed contained an inflatable **paracoita,** and left it at that."

paraphiliac /para FIL ee ak/ n 🕊 A person addicted to unorthodox sexual practices.

"At his first meeting of **Paraphiliacs** Anonymous, Wexler learned that he wasn't the only person in the world to have fallen head over heels for a small Ming vase."
compare **varietist**

parbreak /PAR brake/ v 🕊 To vomit. n 🕊 Vomit.

Parbreaking on the golf course, unfortunately, will do little to lower one's score.
compare **copremesis, hyperemesis**

parnel /par NEL/ n 🕊 The mistress of a priest.

For those men of the cloth for whom a **gugusse** is just not good enough, there is always a **parnel**. Derived via the French from the Latin *Petronilla* (Peter's woman).

"Father Nelson kept promising to leave the faith for

❦ *Pediculous* ❧

his long-suffering **parnel**, but never mustered enough courage to make the move."

compare gugusse

pediculous /ped IK yoo lus/ adj ❧ Afflicted with *pediculosis* (lice infestation); lousy.

"To the great distress of the other parents, Mrs. Willoughby insisted on continuing to send her **pediculous** children to school, insisting 'Lice are nothing, education is everything.'"

peotillomania /*pee o til o MAY nee uh*/ n 🙂 The neurotic habit of constantly pulling at one's penis.

"Although the years of **peotillomania** had been trying ones for both him and his family, Lucien was now the proud possessor of an organ the length of which would be the envy of many a mule."

compare **sacofricosis, trichotillomania**

peotomy /*pee OT o mee*/ n 🙂 Amputation of the penis.

Though most male readers will probably skip quickly over this word, the authors have gone to the trouble of offering a sentence to illustrate this uncomfortably evocative term:

"In a vain attempt to keep his wife from leaving him for another woman, Adam decided to have the **peotomy**."

compare **skoptsy**

phallalgia /*fal AL jee uh*/ n 🙂 Pain in the penis.

Everyone is familiar with the phrase "pain in the ass," but one never hears "pain in the penis" used figuratively—whether because both sexes need a phrase they can identify with, or because it hits too close to home for men, it's hard to be sure.

"With his **phallalgia** increasing by the minute, Edsel bitterly cursed his brothers for dragging him to the bordello the night before."

compare **pudendagra**

phallocrypsis /fal o KRIP sis/ n ❧ Retraction of the penis.

While this word is generally used in a medical sense, it can also describe that greatest of male fears: shrinkage.

"Percy's fondest dream turned into his worst nightmare when he went skinny-dipping with not one, not two, but three luscious young women, only to be dealt a whopping case of **phallocrypsis** by the icy water."

compare **shram**

phalloplasty /FAL o plass tee/ n ❧ Plastic surgery of the penis.

"Oh, how Wesley wished he had never accepted that dare; his penis was horribly twisted now, and no amount of **phalloplasty** could fully restore it."

syn **balanoplasty**

phallorhiknosis /fal or hik NO sis/ n ❧ The shrivelling of the penis with old age.

"Of all the indignities visited upon Philip in his later years—the balding, the bulging waistline, the growing incontinence—it was his **phallorhiknosis** that did the most to obliterate his sense of manhood."

compare **obsolagnium**

philopornist /fie lo PORN ist/ n ❧ An afficionado of prostitutes.

Phallorhiknosis

"The mayor was an avid **philopornist**, much to the consternation of his aides, who seemed to spend most of their time either watching out for the cops or scheduling appointments at private health clinics."
compare **cypripareunia**

pica */PIKE uh/* n ❧ Depraved appetite; hunger for such nonfoods as ashes, clay, starch, chalk, and plaster.

Pilgarlic

Pica has been observed in cases of pregnancy, nutrient deficiency, intestinal worms, and madness.

"The maternity-wear fashion shoot was delayed due to **pica** when the pregnant supermodel began compulsively stuffing her face with handfuls from the playground's sandbox."

pilgarlic */pil GAR lik/* n ~ A sorry-looking bald person.

There are seemingly dozens of words for bald, baldness, and bald people in the English language. All of them are too bloody boring for this book, except **pilgarlic**, which with its "peeled garlic" imagery does have a certain savoir faire.

pinchpin /PINCH pin/ n ✒ A married woman insistent upon her sexual rights; one who demands sex from her husband.

"Prescott wouldn't have minded being married to a **pinchpin** had his newlywed's notion of her rights not included wearing leather and spikes to bed, which made him somewhat . . . well, uncomfortable."

pizzle /PIZZ ul/ n ✒ The penis of a bull, or other large beast, especially when dried to a rubbery consistency and used either to flog people with or as a sexual aid.

Many other languages have similar terms for the penis of a bull, but **pizzle** is nonetheless a distinctly English word. For only the English include a **pizzle's** use as a whipping instrument with its general definition.

Nothing like a good **pizzle** after tea and crumpets, what?

"Despite the consequent rash of whippings, Alderman Wheal's approval ratings soared after he had the police batons replaced with **pizzles**."

compare **byental**

pleonexia /plee o NEX ee uh/ n ✒ Insane greed.

"The trick-or-treating children eventually learned not to ring the doorbell of Mr. Gifford, the stock trader, whose **pleonexia** was so great that instead of giving candy he often took it away."

plooky /*PLOO kee*/ adj ❧ Covered with pimples.

"The designer started a bold new trend in fashion advertising with his decision to hire only the **plookiest** adolescent models."

podobromhidrosis /*po do brome hid RO sis*/ n ❧ Smelly feet.

"Reasoning that it was better to be an oddball than a pariah, Terry began dunking his feet in a tub of cologne before leaving the house each morning, so as to mask his chronic and incurable **podobromhidrosis**."

compare **bromidrosis, maschalephidrosis**

polakuiria /*pol ok YOO ree uh*/ n ❧ An exceedingly frequent need to urinate.

A disorder seemingly confined to just two groups of people: those trying to fall asleep while lying comfortably in their beds, and small children in automobiles.

syn **micturition**
compare **nocturia**

polymasthus /*polly MASS thus*/ n ❧ A person with *polymastia*: more than the usual number of breasts or nipples.

" 'Estelle wasn't just another dull **polymasthus**,' mused the old ex-carnival geek with a faint and somewhat rueful smile. 'She could really make a sideshow come alive.' "

compare **triorchid**

pornocracy /*pore NOK ruh see*/ n ⚬ Government by whores.

This one comes with a little historical background. The term **pornocracy** was once used by the opponents of Pope Sergius III (A.D. 904–11), regarded as one of the worst and most profligate popes in history. Sergius had a notorious **parnel** named Marozia, who was widely resented for her great influence over the papal court. As a result, some referred to the regime as a **pornocracy**.

A member of a ruling **pornocracy** is called a *pornocrat*.

"Many of those polled said they would prefer a **pornocracy** to their current system, reasoning that at least the whores would be honest about their whoring."

compare **cypripareunia, pornophilist**

potvaliant /*pot VAL ee ent*/ adj ⚬ Bold or brave when drunk; more inclined to fight when inebriated.

This is the proper word for someone with the misplaced confidence that comes from being soused. When it's the whisky talking, it's also the *potvalor*: a phenomenon that encourages people to put their lives in danger, or at least to make complete asses of themselves.

"When he awoke the following afternoon, the last

Potvaliant

thing Pegram could remember was climbing aboard the honky-tonk's mechanical bull in a **potvaliant** frenzy."

priapism /PRY up ism/ n ◦ Painful, constant erection without sexual excitement.

"Mr. Cadwallader searched long and hard for a remedy for his **priapism**, but nothing seemed to work: not cold compresses, not thinking about his tubby aunt Lucinda, not even smacking himself with a steel ruler."

compare **chordee**

proctalgia /prok TAL jee uh/ n ◦ Pain in the anus or rectum.

"Grimacing in pain as she reached for the bathroom tissue, Vera wondered whether the triple-jalapeno omelet of the night before had been worth this attack of morning **proctalgia**."

syn pygalgia, rectalgia

pronovalent /*pro NO vuh lent*/ n ⮞ Only able to have sex while lying down.

"In a desperate attempt to spice up their moribund sex life, the Wilsons tried hypnosis, acupuncture, and an adjustable bed, but Mr. Wilson's **pronovalence** simply could not be overcome."

compare stasivalence

pudendagra /*poo DEN duh gruh*/ n ⮞ Pain in the genitals.

"Jasper's only pair of blue jeans were a little tight on him, and after one day at the dude ranch he came down with an incapacitating case of **pudendagra**."

compare phallalgia

pygalgia /*pig AL jee uh*/ n ⮞ Pain in the buttocks.

"Marty was getting his ass kicked so badly in Scrabble, it's a wonder he didn't put down the word **pygalgia**."

compare proctalgia, rectalgia

pygobombe /*PIE go bom*/ n ⮞ A woman with big, sexy buttocks.

From the Greek *pyge* (buttocks) + *bombe* (rounded).

A lovely word. Why say "the bombshell with the

boda-cious bottom," when **pygobombe** is at your disposal?

compare **callipygian, steatopygous**

❧ *Pudendagra* ❧

pygophilous /*pie go FIL us*/ adj ∾ Fond of buttocks.

"To the mixed horror and amusement of the dinner party, Dean, our **pygophilous** adolescent cousin, began telling us all once again that if he were to be reincarnated, he sure hoped to come back as a chair."

compare **mazophilous**

pyriform /*PIH rif orm*/ adj ∾ Pear-shaped.

Pyriform is certainly not the most depraved word in this lexicon. It is, however, perfect for describing a certain depressingly common male physical type: The out-of-shape man whose wide, generous middle tapers to very narrow shoulders.

"Not since the meteor shower had Judy been so forcefully reminded of the power of gravity as at the company picnic full of **pyriform** ad men."

compare **myatonia**

Q

quakebuttock */KWAKE but uk/* n ❧ A trembling coward.

Some compound words, like **bedswerver, smell-smock,** and **quakebuttock,** are special because they convey their meaning by evoking a visual, fairly outrageous action that somehow embodies the spirit of the definition. These words are instantly memorized, and no one ever forgets what they mean. The real reason **quakebuttock** made this book, however, is that the authors were short on good words that start with the letter *q*.

❧ R ❧

rammish /RAM ish/ adj ❧ Strong-smelling, like a ram. Also, lustful, like a ram.

"I'm feeling rather **rammish,** dearie; would you mind terribly much favoring me with a sponge bath?"
compare caprylic, hircine

rantallion /ran TAL ee un/ n ❧ A man or boy whose scrotum hangs lower than his penis.

Or, one "whose shot pouch is longer than the barrel of his piece."—Sir Francis Grose, *1811 Dictionary of the Vulgar Tongue*

rectalgia /rek TAL jee uh/ n ❧ Pain in the rectum.

Yes, there are a few words that mean "pain in the ass." But there are also so many different things in life deserving of this description. For your daily need to describe such pains (be they situations, coworkers, or anything else), you now have an array of options.
syn proctalgia
compare pygalgia

renifleur /*ren uh FLIRRH*/ n ❧ A sexual deviant with an unnatural attraction to body odors, especially urine.

"Clyde was ordered to clean out the latrines for failing to grease his rifle; little did the sergeant know he was sentencing the **renifleur** to his own personal Eden."

see **osphresiophilia**

retifism /*RET if ism*/ n ❧ Foot fetishism.

So-called after the eighteenth-century French fetishist Retif de la Bretonne, who must be glowing with pride from beyond the grave now that his name has been forever linked to this particular sexual aberration. Ah, immortality!

"Felipe had managed to parlay his **retifism** into a nice little career, what with the paid appearances on daytime talk shows; now that the ads in the back of the newspaper were starting to pay off, he could smell a winner."

compare **pageism**

retrocopulation /*ret ro cop yoo LAY shun*/ n ❧ Copulation from behind. Also, copulation between partners facing away from each other in a back-to-back position, as with some animals.

"Stoltzfus tried to convince his scripture-quoting wife that **retrocopulation** was morally acceptable (after all, didn't most of God's creatures do it that way?), but she wouldn't hear of it."

compare **retromingent**

retromingent /ret ro MINJ ent/ adj ∾ Urinating backward, as with some animals.

"George's horse-and-buggy service failed almost immediately after it became apparent that he had purchased a pair of **retromingent** animals."

compare retrocopulation

rhinoplast /RINE o plast/ n ∾ A person who has had rhinoplasty (plastic surgery of the nose).

Rhinoplasty is one hell of an ugly word for an operation that is supposed to beautify. The highly applicable **rhinoplast** is less common, but equally unappealing.

"Jane just couldn't stand yet another cocktail party full of smug and overdressed **rhinoplasts**—not with her own massive honker in full attendance."

rhypophagous /rye POFF uh gus/ adj ∾ Dung-eating.

This one comes from the Greek *rhypos* (filth).

syn: coprophagous, merdivorous, scatophagous, stercovorous

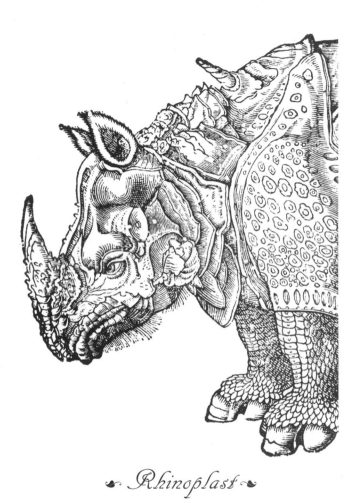

❧ *Rhinoplast* ❧

S

sacofricosis /sak o frik O sis/ n ❧ Habitual rubbing of the genitals through one's pant pocket.

Call it pocket pool, or what you will; even if it is not habitual, every man is prone to a little **sacofricosis** on occasion. Sometimes it is a persistent itch he absolutely must scratch; sometimes a slight adjustment is unavoidable; on occasion he may simply need reassurance that he's still all there. And pockets are so conveniently located, just crying out to be utilized to their full potential.

"Busted during a particularly indelicate flurry of **sacofricosis,** Boyle tried to save face by making a big show of searching for his keys."

sangrado /san GRAH do/ n ❧ A quack; a medical impostor.

The next time you come down with a malady that is *iatrogenic* (caused by doctors), counter your physician's impenetrable jargon by giving him a little honorific of your own.

saprostomus /*sup ROSS tuh muss*/ n ❧ A person with bad breath.

Pity the **saprostomus,** for though he makes others choke, he himself suffers ostracization, and he knows not why. From the Greek *sapros* (putrid) + *stoma* (mouth).

" 'Why didn't you tell me before?' cried Jim the **saprostomus** between sobs, as his friends and family brought their bad-breath intervention to a climax."

compare **bromopnea**

satyriasis /*sat ih RYE uh sis*/ n ❧ Maniacal lustfulness in males.

This condition is named after those horny capripedes the *satyrs,* perpetually erect goat-men of ancient myth.

compare **contrectation, erotomania, lascivia, tentigo**

saulie /*SAW lee*/ n ❧ A hired mourner at a funeral.

Oh, humanity.

"First the expense of the undertaker's bill, then the marble tomb, now the **saulies** holding out for more money; Eidelfilch's widow thanked the Lord that her husband, while unpopular, had at least been stinking rich."

compare **claqueur**

scambler /*SKAM blur*/ n ❧ One who drops in uninvited at dinner time in the hope of getting free food.

"An inveterate **scambler,** Otis knew who ate early and

who dined late; when he was on his game he could time his visits closely enough so as to **scamble** at least three dinners in one day."

syn **smellfeast**

compare **groak**

scaphism /SKAFF ism/ n ➤ The practice of covering a victim in honey and strapping him in to a hollow tree exposed to stinging insects, in order to inflict a lingering death.

"Ferdinand was an excellent torturer, and a tireless self-promoter as well; just that morning he had sent placards to all the local inquisitors reading "Thumbscrews not working? Why not give **scaphism** a try? Affordable rates. Group discounts.' "

compare **bastinado, ganch**

scatophage /SKAT o faj/ n ➤ An eater of excrement.

Other words for this include **merdivore** and **coprophagist**.

"When Eunice found out that halitosis was to blame, she breathed a sigh of relief, for in her heart of hearts she had always harbored the suspicion that her husband was a closet **scatophage**."

scatophagous /skat OFF uh gus/ adj ➤ Feeding on excrement.

syn **coprophagous, merdivorous, rhypophagous, stercovorous**

❧ *Scopophilia* ❧

scopophilia /*skope uh FIL ee uh*/ n ❧ Sexual interest in erotic imagery, especially when used as a substitute for actual sex.

"Being struck suddenly blind would have taxed any man, but for Mr. Bigelow, with his acute **scopophilia,** it smacked of divine vengeance."

scoracrasia /*skore uh KRAY zhuh*/ n ❧ Involuntary defecation.

"Wedding jitters? Maybe. Whatever the cause, Jill's prenuptial **scoracrasia** was rapidly becoming cause for alarm."

syn **copracrasia, encopresis**

screation /*skree AY shun*/ n ～ Neurotic and excessive hawking and clearing of the throat.

"Following as it did his weekly act of **irrumation**, Comstock's wife's prolonged **screation** did little to enhance his blissful afterglow."

shardborn /*SHARD born*/ adj ～ Born or residing in excrement.

"How long would the greatest political mistake of his career keep coming back to haunt him? After all, it was decades ago that he had made the infamous comment about the '**shardborn** Okies.' "

syn **fimiculous**

sharny /*SHAR nee*/ adj ～ Befouled with dung.

It is one of the great mysteries of the English language: Why do we have so many words for spraying (or getting sprayed) with shit? Does it actually happen that often? Or did the lexicographers of yesteryear amuse themselves by seeing who could come up with the best word for this horrid idea?

At last count there seemed to be at least a dozen such words. In the interest of scholastic thoroughness, the authors have included the seven they found most interesting: **beray, bescumber, conskite, immerd, ordured, sharny,** and **shitten**.

"Kelly was all for celebrating his ethnic heritage, but when it came to kissing the **Sharny** Stone, he balked."

syn ordured, shitten

shitten /SHIT en/ adj ❧ Covered with or stained by feces.

"Meredith hated to make a fuss, but when her clothes came back **shitten** a second time, she resolved to have a word with the lady at the laundromat."

syn ordured, sharny
compare beray, bescumber, conskite, immerd

shram /SHRAM/ v ❧ To shrivel or become numb from cold.

"As a movie star, Desmond's vanity knew no bounds, and he would have been tickled pink by the nude photos flooding the Internet had they not been taken when he was so unflatteringly **shrammed** from swimming."

compare phallocrypsis

sialoquent /sigh AL o kwent/ adj ❧ Apt to spray saliva when speaking.

One can always "compliment" a blustering or pompous speaker by referring to him as extremely **sialoquent**.

"All the the other seats were taken, so Amanda had no choice but to sit front and center, grit her teeth, and endure two hours of dehumanizing misting from Mr. Fletcher, the **sialoquent** history professor."

compare **conspue, sputative**

skoptsy /SKOPT zee/ n, pl ∾ An eighteenth-century breakaway Russian religious sect whose members castrated themselves out of an extreme devotion to sexual abstinence.

That must have taken a lot of balls.

compare **peotomy**

slubberdegullion /slub er dee GULL yun/ n ∾ A contemptible slob.

"Mr. Roth had a normal—if slightly dishevelled—appearance, and if it weren't for the odor of spoiled milk that followed him everywhere, no one would have guessed that at home he was a complete **slubberdegullion**."

smatchet /SMACH it/ n ∾ A small and nasty person.

"Bridget hated the game of spin the bottle; whenever her turn came around, the bottle would invariably come to rest pointing directly at Billy, the **smatchet** with the bad teeth."

smegma /SMEG muh/ n ∾ A cheesy, foul-smelling material found under the foreskin of the penis and near the clitoris.

From the Greek *smegma* (soap).

Smegma is one of the better-known words in this lexicon. It also happens to be one of the more disgusting.

smellfeast /*SMELL feast*/ n ☙ A mealtime moocher.

"It was squat and fat, with nostrils big enough to fit both thumbs, but to Ludwig the **smellfeast** his nose was his greatest asset."

syn **scambler**

smellsmock /*SMELL smock*/ n ☙ A revolting lecher.

"When the news came out about Mr. Wilburn, Janet couldn't believe that the kindly old pushbroom who always opened the door for her was actually an inveterate **smellsmock** who exposed himself to schoolgirls."

snurt /*SNURT*/ v ☙ To eject mucus from the nose when sneezing.

"A bright child, Granville might have had a promising future in life, had he not **snurted** on the class bully that grim day while in line at the lunch counter."

sophomania /*soff o MAY nee uh*/ n ☙ The delusion that one is wise.

An unattractive and widespread condition that does not discriminate on the basis of race, class, color, or creed; some degree of which has bewitched everyone from the guy on the bus filling in the Wonderword to the inventor of colored cling wrap.

compare **witling**

sordes /*sore DEES*/ n, pl ⁓ Filthy, dark deposits that accumulate on the teeth and lips, consisting of foul, dried stomach secretions.

Yet another revolting medical term you probably had no idea existed. Isn't your life a little bit richer for the thought that someday you might wind up in a hospital bed with a tube up your nose and **sordes** on your lips?

sorn /*SORN*/ v ⁓ To sponge off of friends for room and board.

Some people are born to **sorn**; therein lies their greatest talent.

sorner /*SORE ner*/ n ⁓ One who sorns; one who imposes on the hospitality of another for room and board.

Originally, **sorner** was a legal term, referring to a type of criminal miscreant who procured food or lodging for himself through the use of force or menace. Now it applies to miscreants who take advantage of their friends.

"Basil changed his locks and his phone number when he learned his apartment had been given a three-star rating in *The **Sorner's** Guide to New York City*."

compare **scambler, smellfeast**

spermatorrhea /*SPUR mat o REE uh*/ n ∾ The abnormal leaking of semen through the penis without orgasm.

"Chadwick had taken to masturbating five or six times a day, hoping to rid himself of enough sperm to get out of wearing the diapers that had been prescribed for his severe **spermatorrhea**."

compare **aspermia, spermatoschesis**

spermatoschesis /*SPUR mat o SKEE sis*/ n ∾ The suppression of ejaculation.

It is difficult for most men to imagine **spermatoschesis** unnaccompanied by some sort of acute pain.

"Molesworth had always prided himself on his powers of **spermatoschesis**—and rightfully so—but on this most inopportune of occasions it had failed him."

compare **aspermia, spermatorrhea**

spintry /*SPIN tree*/ n ∾ A male prostitute.

Considering how many different words for *female* prostitute one has to wade through during a typical hour of dictionary-reading, it is a blatant injustice that there are not more words like **spintry** (for more on this, see **franion**).

"The jobless lexicographer reached for a pencil when he read this ad in the Help Wanted section: 'Wanted: **Spintry**. Excellent pay, benefits. Must have experience, references. Flexible hours.' Alas, he had no references."

compare **gugusse, gunsel, urning**

spoffokins */SPOFF uh kins/* n 🦆 A prostitute posing as a wife.

"It was a slow night at the No-Tell Motel: just a couple of **spoffokins** and their bashful johns."

compare **parnel**

spraints */SPRAINTS/* n, pl 🦆 Otter feces.

An odd but memorable word. The challenge, of course, is to somehow work it into everyday conversation without sounding strained. Good luck.

"Charlie got a sprained elbow from constantly skimming the **spraints** from his swimming pool after a family of endangered otters took up residence there."

sputative */SPEW tuh tiv/* adj 🦆 Prone to spitting; liable to spit.

One of a mere handful of words in the English language that apply in equal measure to llamas and baseball players.

compare **conspue, sialoquent**

stasivalence */stuh SIV uh lence/* n 🦆 The state of only being able to have sex while standing.

"Clark's **stasivalence** was so pronounced, and his wife so much taller than he, that he often found himself in the embarrassing position of wearing high heels during love play."

compare **pronovalent**

steatopygous /stee at OP ig us/ adj 🦢 Fat-assed.

Scattered throughout this book are words like **steatopygous,** which are useful in those situations when one wishes to make crass comments about the anatomy of members of the opposite sex without risking being understood by the wrong person. Just remember to familiarize your friends with these words beforehand, to avoid the awkwardness of having to define them on the spot. Then you can speak freely in an impenetrable code.

compare **callipygian, dasypygal**

steatorrhea /stee at o REE uh/ n 🦢 Frothy, stinking excrement that floats, due to an abnormally high fat content.

Steatorrhea is also pale, greasy, and hard to flush. This shit is really disgusting.

compare **allochezia, lientery**

stercoraceous /STIR kuh RAY shuss/ adj 🦢 Of or pertaining to dung.

syn **fecaloid, ordurous**

stercorary /STIR kuh rare ee/ n 🦢 A place for storing dung.

"Mrs. Swinton was hardly a meddlesome landlady, but when one of her tenants decided to rent out his spare room as a **stercorary** for local farmers, she felt it was time to put her foot down."

compare **urinarium**

stercoverous /*ster KOV er us*/ adj ✒ Dung-eating.

"We were all fond of the Henderson's dog—he was an affable pooch—but he had the disagreeable combination of being both insatiably **stercovorous** and inclined to lick one's face."

syn **coprophagous, merdivorous, rhypophagous, scatophagous**

sthenolagnia /*sthen uh LAG nee uh*/ n ✒ Sexual excitement in a woman arising from a display of strength or prowess.

"When Sally pushed him off the bed and barked 'Gimme twenty,' Hal realized that dating a girl with **sthenolagnia** was a lot like boot camp."

stomatomenia /*STO mat o MEE nee uh*/ n ✒ Bleeding from the mouth during menstruation.

The only solace for those readers traumatized by the definition of **stomatomenia** (and it is completely awful) is that the blood flow in question is not, obviously, redirected from the uterus. It is a separate, but simultaneous, flow of blood.

"While it pained Abigail immensely to cancel her date with the handsome Mr. Gladstone, she simply couldn't go out—not with her **stomatomenia** as bad as it was."

compare **bromomenorrhea**

suggilate /*SUG il ate*/ v ✒ To beat black and blue.

A whole phrase in one word. **Suggilate** is more

❧ Suggilate ❧

specific and evocative than everyday words like *thrash, batter,* and *pummel.* Plus, it just sounds like it has punch. Saying you'd like to **suggilate** someone is a satisfying way to express your feelings of aggression and hostility.

compare **fustigate**

suoid */SYOO oid/* adj ❧ Hoglike.

Suoid is different from the better-known *porcine*

✌ *Suoid* ✌

(piglike) in that it refers to *hogs*: bigger, fatter, and greedier than plain old pigs.

"Dexter didn't know if the two were connected, but after the surgery left him with a heart valve from a pig, he caught himself making love with distinctly **suoid** sqealings and gruntings."

compare blattoid

suppalpation /*sup pal PAY shun*/ n ✌ The act of winning by fondling. Also, wheedling or coaxing.

In other words, stroking one's way to success.

compare contrectation

syndyasmian /*sin die AZ mee an*/ adj ✌ Pertaining to promiscuous sexual pairing, or to the temporary cohabitation of couples.

Finally, a word of dignity and charm with which to describe that much-maligned event: the one-night stand.

"No one in his family ever mentioned that dark day when Mr. Bradley quit his job, sold the car, and ran off to join a **syndyasmian** cult in California."

T

tarassis /*tuh RASS iss*/ n ❧ Male hysteria.

A curiously broad definition; perhaps even a little vague. For a mania that might fall under this heading, and one potential cause of **tarassis,** check the entry for **micromania**.

tenesmus /*ten EZ mus*/ n ❧ Painful, spasmodic attempts to urinate or defecate, accompanied by involuntary straining.

It's that bit about "involuntary straining" that makes **tenesmus** uniquely unpleasant to contemplate.

"Grace felt nothing but sympathy for her husband during his racking bout with **tenesmus,** but she had to admit that the constant straining had helped him work off more than a few unnecessary pounds."

compare **nisus**

tentigo /*ten TIE go*/ n ❧ Excessive lust; inordinate desire for sex.

Not to be confused with *impetigo,* a rash you get at the

beach, although both can be discomfiting conditions for a man in a tight bathing suit.

syn **erotomania, lascivia**

compare **satyriasis**

thelypthoric /*thel ip THOR ik*/ adj 🐦 Morally corruptive to women.

A fairly cryptic definition; the authors wish their sources could be a bit more specific.

"As a young man and budding debaucher of women, Stanley had decided to make a study of all things **thelypthoric**. Consequently, he was blind from syphilis by the age of thirty."

tomalley /*tuh MOLL ee*/ n 🐦 The green, slimy liver of a cooked lobster.

There are, incidentally, two types of people in the world: those who like **tomalley,** and those who don't especially care for ill-smelling, mucuslike substances harvested from the innards of animals.

"After Mrs. Pendergrast reiterated her pronouncement about the **tomalley** being the 'best part' of the lobster, little Joe insisted she take his in return for both claws."

tribade /*trib ADE*/ n 🐦 A woman, especially one with a large clitoris, who practices tribadism; a female genital rubber.

Tribade is a word with a long and worthy pedigree. In

the first century A.D., the famed Roman poet Martial wrote: "Philaenis the **tribade** pedicates* boys, and stiffer than a man in one day work eleven girls."

compare **fricatrice**

tribadism /TRIB ud ism/ n ❧ Genital rubbing between women. Also, any rubbing of the female genitalia that results in orgasm.

Tribadism comes from the Greek *tribas* (rubbing).

"Denise thanked heaven her parents had sent her to horseback riding camp as a little girl, or else she might never have stumbled upon the joys of **tribadism** when learning how to canter that fateful afternoon."

trichotillomania /TRIK o til o MAY nee uh/ n ❧ The tearing out of one's own hair, as in certain disordered states of mind.

Everyday events that may drive one to **trichotillomania** include locking oneself out of one's car and leaving one's plane ticket on the dresser while one speeds to the airport.

"The **trichotillomania** first appeared not long after Prescott filled in his ticket wrong and missed the lottery jackpot by a single digit—it had never completely gone away since."

*****Pedicate**: To debauch via the anus.

triorchid /*try OR kid*/ n 🐟 A man with three testicles. Also, figuratively, an extremely lascivious man.

"Born with 'one to spare,' Gustav, the alcoholic **triorchid**, enjoyed telling everyone within earshot exactly how it felt to be one of the horniest men alive."

compare **polymasthus**

troat /*TROAT*/ v 🐟 To cry out like a rutting buck. n 🐟 The cry of a rutting buck.

The authors know of no better word for a bellowing mating call.

"Mortified, Winchester realized he had shattered the predawn silence—and awoken everyone in the lodge—by **troating** during the act of love."

🐟 *Trocar* 🐟

trocar /*TRO kar*/ n 🐟 A hollow tube farmers insert into the rectums of cattle to release trapped gas.

To be sure, **trocars,** which at first glance resemble

handheld drills, do have other uses, such as the draining of liquid from body cavities. But nothing quite as humorous as deflating steers.

"One of little Timmy's least favorite chores on the farm was buggering the stud bull with a **trocar** every afternoon."

troilism /*TROY lism*/ n ❧ Sex between three partners; *ménage à trois*.

Troilism comes from the French *trois* (three). Which begs the question: why are the English words for so many sexual concepts **(frottage, renifleur, retifism)** so often French-derived? And where along the line did English speakers decide to attach the word "French" ("French toast," "French kiss," "French tickler") to anything that was either sexy or tasted good? Do the French, like blondes, have more fun, or do we just like to think that they do?

"Smitty was overjoyed that his wife had finally agreed to partake in **troilism** for his thirtieth birthday—until he saw that her choice of a third was the hairy plumber from downstairs."

Troilism

U

unnun /un NUN/ v 🙥 To strip a nun of her position or character.

While the strict definition of this word doesn't specify that it involves engaging in sex with a nun, we are left to ask: How else would one strip a nun of her character—encourage her to gamble? And while the deviants reading this book will in all probability never have a chance to **unnun** a holy sister, now at least they can fantasize about it with the correct terminology.

"When Pablo's sweetheart joined the convent he refused to acknowledge defeat, but spent the rest of his days dreaming up futile schemes to **unnun** her."

uranism /YOO run ism/ n 🙥 Homosexuality among "physically normal" men.

The authors' source does not specify exactly what is meant by "physically normal."

"Sutton's doctoral thesis, '**Uranism** in the Prison System: Past, Present, and Future' yielded him the bene-

❧ *Annun* ❧

fit of a small degree of public acclaim—and a surfeit of phone numbers from strapping ex-convicts."

urinarium /YOO rin AIR ee um/ n ✒ A tank that collects the runoff urine from a stable and stores it for future use.

Urine collected in this way could then be used for fertilizer, or perhaps even for **lant** or **lotium**.

"As punishment for breaking the eggs, the bossman ordered Oliver to swab out the farm's **urinarium** in the noon heat."

compare **stercorary**

urinous /YOO rin us/ adj ✒ Smelling like, marked by the presence of, or resembling urine.

A word as useful in the big city as it is on the farm.

"The slight **urinous** tinge to the soup was the tipoff that eventually led to the arrest of the vengeful caterer."

compare **fecaloid**

urning /URN ing/ n ✒ A homosexual.

An uncommon but fairly straightforward word for someone who isn't straight.

"Johnny Flowers, cabaret star extraordinaire, changed into yet another sequined outfit—his third for the evening—and regaled the sold-out crowd with his emotional torch song 'I've Got a Yearning for an **Urning**.' "

urolagnia /*YOO ro LAG nee uh*/ n ☙ Sexual excitement from urine or urination, either one's own or another's.

"Few fans enjoyed drinking quart after quart of warm beer at the ballpark as much as Troy, whose **urolagnia** also made the trip to the men's room every other inning a keenly-awaited treat."

urolagniac /*YOO ro LAG nee ak*/ n ☙ A deviant who derives sexual pleasure from urine or urination, his own or another person's.

"Medcorp executives prayed to God that the press wouldn't catch wind of that little business concerning Fred, the **urolagniac** lab assistant, and his nocturnal bacchanals."

compare **renifleur**

urticate /*URT ik ate*/ v ☙ To flog with stinging nettles: a form of treatment for paralysis.

"Mr. Witherspoon enjoyed a good, stiff **urtication** in the morning, and whenever possible would follow it up by sacking one or two members of his staff."

compare **mastigophoric**

uxoravalent /*ooks or AHV uh lent*/ adj ☙ Able to have sex only with one's wife.

It is unclear why we need a word for such a rare condition. There is no real explanation, other than the fact that lexicographers like to have all their bases covered.

compare uxorovalent

uxorious /ooks OR ee us/ adj ᔉ Overly fond of one's wife.

Uxorious describes the man who dotes on and idolizes his wife to sickening excess.

"His coworkers finally dropped a piano on Harlan, the **uxorious** moving man, when he said he was taking a third job so he could afford music lessons for his tonedeaf bride."

uxorovalent /ooks or O vuh lent/ adj ᔉ Able to have sex only with someone *other* than one's wife.

Oh, what a difference a letter makes.

compare uxoravalent

V

vagient /VAY *jee ent*/ adj ❧ Crying like a child.

"Sensing that his political life hung in the balance, the president went on national TV and made a **vagient** speech in which he admitted to every sin he had committed since the third grade."

vaginismus /*vaj in IZ mus*/ n ❧ Spasmodic tightening of the muscles around the vagina, resulting from an extreme aversion to penetration.

"Zelda's date had a great sense of humor and beautiful eyes, but something about the way he ate the bratwurst triggered violent **vaginismus** in her."

compare **colpoxerosis**

valgus /VAL *gus*/ n ❧ A bowlegged person.

"Tony, the pint-sized **valgus,** had all the physical tools of a champion goat jockey. All he lacked was the desire."

varietist /*ver EYE uh tist*/ n ❧ A person with unorthodox appetites.

"The marriage that had started out so well was doomed to fail, for she was a **varietist,** and he more of a meat-and-potatoes kind of lover."

compare paraphiliac

vernalagnia /vern uh LAG nee uh/ n ～ Heightened sexual desire in the springtime.

In other words, spring fever. A disease with only one known cure . . . a long, cold shower.

compare nisus

viraginity /vih ruh JIN it ee/ n ～ Manliness in a woman.

Viraginity has no etymological connection to "virginity," and although the adjectival form of this word is *viraginian,* there is nothing in the literature to indicate that the condition is not equally common in Arkansas or North Carolina.

Viraginity loosely describes the attributes of a *virago* (originally a strong female warrior, later a bold, impudent woman). All three words stem from the Latin *vir* (man).

"Lucy read the warning on the diet pills and figured she was safe: after all, how bad could '**viraginity**' be? As a result, her once-ample chest now resembled that of a slightly overweight ten-year-old boy."

compare gynander

vomiturition /VOM ich yoor ISH un/ n ～ Vomiting with violent spasms but little brought up. Also, repeated unproductive vomiting.

❧ *Viraginity* ❧

"When his attorney told him just how much the divorce was going to cost him, Mr. Pecksniff fell victim to a prolonged bout of **vomiturition**."

compare **keck**

W

wamble /*WOM bul*/ v ❧ To heave and roll, as an upset stomach; also, to rumble in the stomach, as hard-to-digest food.

"Three hot dogs and two ice creams later, my poor stomach was **wambling** as it had never **wambled** before."

compare **collywobbles**

witling /*WIT ling*/ n ❧ A person who lacks understanding or intelligence.

"Günter, the leader of the dangerous expedition to the high Andes, was an imposing man with an air of imperturbable confidence about him; unfortunately—as everyone was about to discover—he was also a world-class **witling**."

compare **mumchance**

wittol /*WIT all*/ n ❧ A contented cuckold; a man unbothered by his wife's infidelity.

"Gregor the **wittol** breathed a sigh of relief. The months of tension in bed, the tedious arguments every

❧ *Wittol* ❧

154

night, the awkward and unsatisfying sex—all these were things of the past, now that the virile Fernando had moved in next door."

compare **lenocinium**

X⋅Y⋅Z

xanthodont /*ZAN thoh dont*/ adj ❧ Having yellow teeth.

A distinguishing characteristic of smokers and coffee drinkers.

"Baking soda, rinses, bleach: none of it worked. Only the airbrush could help Natalie, the **xanthodont** fashion model."

xysma /*ZIZE muh*/ n ❧ "Material, like bits of membrane, found in the stools of diarrhea," according to *Webster's Universal Unabridged Dictionary* of 1936. (We thought it best not to tinker with this one.)

However could this charming word have fallen into disuse? It is definitely one of the most revolting entries in any dictionary—and you had to make it all the way to the *X*s for it. Think of it as a little reward for getting this far.
compare **lientery**

zooerastia /*zoo er ASS tee uh*/ n ❧ The practice of engaging in sexual activity with an animal.

"Father Rick could never remember whether **zooeras-tia** was a mortal sin or a venial one, so he told the man in the confessional to say twenty Hail Marys and made a mental note to pray for the man's soul."

A SELECT BIBLIOGRAPHY

The American Heritage Dictionary of the English Language. Boston: Houghton Mifflin Company, 1980.

The American Illustrated Medical Dictionary. 9th ed. Philadelphia and London: W. B. Saunders Company, 1918.

Black's Law Dictionary. 4th ed. St. Paul, Minn.: West Publishing Company, 1951.

Black's Medical Dictionary. 35th ed. Totowa, N.J.: Barnes & Noble Books, 1987.

Bowler, Peter. *The Superior Person's Book of Words.* New York: Dell Laurel, 1982.

Brent, Irwin M. and Rod L. Evans. *More Weird Words.* New York: Berkley Books, 1995.

Byrne, Josefa Heifitz. *Mrs. Byrne's Dictionary of Unusual, Obscure, and Preposterous Words.* New York: Citadel Press and University Books, 1974.

The Century Dictionary and Cyclopedia. New York: Century Company, 1889–1914.

The Compact Oxford English Dictionary. 2d ed. Oxford: Oxford University Press, 1991.

Davies, T. Lewis. *A Supplementary Glossary.* London: George Bell and Sons, 1881.

Dickson, Paul. *Words.* New York: Delacorte Press, 1982.

Dictionary of Psychology. 3d British Commonwealth ed. London: Peter Owen, 1972.

Ehrlich, Eugene. *The Highly Selective Dictionary for the Extraordinarily Literate.* New York: HarperCollins Publishers, 1997.

Elster, Charles Harrington. *There's a Word for It!* New York: Pocket Books, 1986.

Funk & Wagnall's New Standard Dictionary of the English Language. Medallion edition. New York: Funk & Wagnall's Company, 1942.

Grambs, David. *Dimboxes, Epopts, and Other Quidams.* New York: Workman Publishing, 1986.

———. *The Endangered English Dictionary.* New York: W. W. Norton & Company, 1994.

Grose, Francis. *1811 Dictionary of the Vulgar Tongue.* London: Bibliophile Books, 1984.

Halliwell, James Orchard. *Dictionary of Archaic Words.* London: Bracken Books, 1989.

Hellweg, Paul. *The Insomniac's Dictionary*. New York: Ballantine Books, 1986.

Hinsie, Leland E. and Robert Campbell. *Psychiatric Dictionary.* New York: Oxford University Press, 1960.

Hook, J. N. *The Grand Panjandrum*. New York: Macmillan Publishing Company, 1980.

Johnson, Samuel. *A Dictionary of the English Language*. London: William Bell, 1783.

Kacirk, Jeffrey. *Forgotten English*. New York: William Morrow & Company, 1997.

Lempriere, J. *Lempriere's Classical Dictionary*. London: Millner and Company, 1887.

The Merck Manual of Diagnosis and Therapy. 15th ed. Rahway, N.J.: Merck & Co., 1987.

Nare, Robert. *Nare's Glossary*. Charles Loeffler, 1825.

Partridge, Eric. *A Dictionary of Slang and Unconventional English.* New York: Macmillan Publishing Company, 1961.

———. *Origins: A Short Etymological Dictionary of Modern English*. New York: Macmillan Publishing Company, 1958.

Psychiatric Dictionary. 3d ed. New York: Oxford University Press, 1960.

Q.P.B. Dictionary of Difficult Words. New York: Quality Paperback Book Club, 1994.

Rheingold. Howard. *They Have a Word for It*. Los Angeles: Jeremy P. Tarcher, 1988.

Rodale, Jerome Irving. *The Synonym Finder*. Emmaus, Pa.: Rodale Press, 1978.

Schmidt, J. E. *The Lecher's Lexicon*. New York: Bell Publishing Company, 1967.

Schur, Norman W. *1000 Most Obscure Words*. New York: Facts on File, 1990.

Sharman, Julian. *A Cursory History of Swearing*. New York: Burt Franklin, 1968.

Shipley, Joseph T. *Dictionary of Early English*. Paterson, N.J.: Littlefield, Adams, and Company, 1963.

The Signet/Mosby Medical Encyclopedia. New York: Penguin Books, 1987.

Tabor's Cyclopedic Medical Dictionary. 15th ed. Philadelphia: F. A. Davis Company, 1985.

Warrack, Alexander. *The Concise Scots Dictionary*. Poole Dorset: New Orchard Editions, 1988.

Webster's New International Dictionary. 2d ed. Springfield, Mass.: G. & C. Merriam Company, 1946.

Webster's Third New International Dictionary. Springfield, Mass.: G. & C. Merriam Company, 1961.

Webster's Universal Unabridged Dictionary. Merriam-Webster, 1936.

Webster, Noah, *An American Dictionary of the English Language.* Springfield. Mass.: George and Charles Merriam, 1857.

Willy, Vander, and Fisher, *The Illustrated Encyclopedia of Sex.* New York: Cadillac Publishing Company, 1950.